STOP IT SWAP IT

How to Short-Circuit the Negativity Spiral in **10 Seconds or Less**

By: Emma Romano & Bradley Ramacher

SIBRA HOUSE

A catalogue record for this work is available from the National Library of Australia

ISBN: 978-1-7645728-0-4

Why we've created this book…

We want this information accessible to everyone.

Our goal is to raise the frequency of this planet by delivering deeply powerful knowledge in a simple but effective way.

This material promotes empowerment, healing, self-elevation and practical manifestation. You, my friend, have the absolute power to shape the life you envision and deserve.

Let's change your life.

Let's lift our collective vibration.

Let's do it together!

Contents

For my family, friends and you. ~ Emma

**For all those who have forgotten how powerful
they *really* are. ~ Bradley**

'If you don't step forward, you're always in the same place.'
~ Nora Roberts

My Story

From Then To Now

Change often begins with a single instance of realisation. It's all we need to jumpstart a new habit or way of living—a lightbulb moment in the mind that illuminates a pathway we didn't or couldn't see.

Mine came in 2014 when, outwardly, my life looked amazing. I had a great husband, two wonderful sons, legendary friends, a pleasant home in Melbourne, an active job as a tennis coach and a secondary role at a chiropractic clinic. I competed in tennis, netball and roller derby, working hard and playing harder. Life *should* have had me riding waves of happiness. My interior *should* have matched my exterior.

But here's what was really going on.

Inside, I'd unravelled. I was in pain and full of negativity. I'd become toxic. Fake. Consumed by denial. Broken. My internal conversations were disparaging, judgmental and brimmed with self-loathing. As a do-it-all type of perfectionist, I flip-flopped between mania and daily burnout. My way of life was 'all go, no rest'. I couldn't help but compare myself to everyone else or compete with them. I avoided my emotions by drinking heavily and ignored the consequences of my insane lifestyle. Our family unit had fractured to such a degree that I thought it was beyond repair. To put it simply, I was an absolute mess.

It was on an Easter camping trip that year when I started to lose my eyesight. Sitting in the car with my family, as we headed to meet the friends we were holidaying with, my left eye went blurry and watery. When I looked into the distance, nothing was clear. My husband, who is seven years younger, joked, 'You're just getting old, baby.'

As we approached camp, I shrugged off my discomfort, putting it down to exhaustion. The following day, my colour vision vanished. A sharp pain shot through my head whenever I moved my eye back and forth or up and down. My body ached, as if I were on the verge of a stomach flu.

Five days later, I found myself in the hospital.

Forty-eight hours after that, I'd gone entirely blind in my left eye.

As the pain in my head grew unbearable, hospital staff took notice. A quick scan revealed I had a swollen optic nerve all the way to my brain.

And just like that, I was diagnosed with optic neuritis.

That was when my husband shut down. He couldn't mentally or emotionally handle his wife being sick. He withdrew and fell into deep denial, furthering the damage our ruptured household was already taking. His emotional absence filled me with dense, anxiety-inducing panic. Thank God I had my amazing mum for support.

My doctor explained that they'd have to run some tests, but there were three known causes for developing optic neuritis: a brain tumour, HIV/AIDS and multiple sclerosis (MS). They reassured me by saying that this solitary event was nothing to worry about, but my mind spiralled with what-if scenarios. I could confidently rule out HIV/AIDS, and what I knew about MS was only what I'd seen on television, where people in wheelchairs had lost control of their bodies. That left 'brain tumour' as my perceived worst outcome.

After an agonising three-day wait, I was back at the hospital for test results, and, ever the drama queen, I was in full meltdown mode. Standing in the oncology wing, surrounded by grey walls and grey linoleum and grey chairs and grey desks and a dozen posters of men and women in wheelchairs, I howled in despair. Was this what I had to look forward to? Was this it?

On April 10 at 11 am, the neurologist greeted me, sat me down and delivered the news: they'd found three lesions on my brain and brain stem.

I had MS.

My reaction to the diagnosis was to rush home and down a bottle of sauvignon blanc. It devastated me. No one beyond my mum, husband and best friend knew, and I kept it that way. In isolation, I got sucked into the story of my diagnosis and fully agreed to a new life with it.

It was the worst thing I could've done.

Hospital visits soon became my norm. I struggled to heal from both the optic neuritis and MS. I received intravenous medication every two days, with no effect. I wasn't healing. These days, I get why: I had worked my many diagnoses into my beliefs, agreements and identity. They'd become an actual part of *me*.

Six weeks passed before I suffered another event, this time at work— my leg went numb from hip to foot. In a matter of seconds, I'd lost all feeling. The hospital started me on a heavy medication that the nurse warned was known to cause suicidal thoughts, depression and chronic fatigue. And I did it again. I adopted those side effects into my identity with the first tablet I swallowed. I just believed I had them.

Did I *really*? Yes.

But from the medication? Not likely.

Back then, what I failed to understand about identity was how profoundly it can affect reality. Since I was consistently thinking, feeling, speaking about and acting as if I had these new conditions, I did. I had no clue my body was responding to my thoughts and feelings, or that my cells were listening to everything I said and did.

But more on that later.

Instead, things just weren't adding up. As the medications intensified, my depression worsened, and I went down like a bucket of shit. I found myself growing increasingly lost.

Three short months into my diagnosis, I'd deteriorated to a shadow of who I was previously. I existed in deep states of sadness, suffering and horrendous health. I could no longer work or drive. I couldn't be a mother to my boys. I'd lost feeling in other areas of my body, including my face, chest, arms and left foot—all accompanying my still-numb right leg. Getting around was a stomach-churning experience of shuffling, numbness and fatigue. My trek from bed to couch and couch to bed became my only exercise. I was blind in my left eye. Whatever I couldn't see or feel, I dropped. My short-term memory diminished to the point where I couldn't recall conversations I'd just been a part of.

Despite all of this, I didn't acknowledge the gravity of the situation until I nearly caused a serious accident. At a family gathering, my husband passed me our eighteen-month-old niece to hold.

And… I dropped her.

Inches from her head striking the concrete step, my husband caught and swept her away from harm. I was indescribably horrified.

My best friend helped me visit a neurologist the very next day.

The doctor put me through a sensory test where I lay down blindfolded while they pricked me with a needle, checking my body for sensation. As I lay there in the dark, my friend cracked jokes and kept me laughing.

After a while, I got impatient, pulled off the blindfold and asked, 'When are you going to start?' The doctor was hovering over me, and my friend had tears streaming down her face.

They'd already completed the test. I hadn't felt a thing.

The doctor instructed me to go home and prepare the house for a wheelchair, giving me six months before I'd need one permanently. He guessed that I'd end up in a nursing home within two years.

I thought, *at forty-six?* Nah, I don't think so.

I stood up and said, 'Fuck that!'

It was the best decision I've *ever* made.

Realising this Miracle Process

I asked myself an incredibly difficult question: *What if I gave this to myself?*

And I'm eternally grateful for facing this possibility because it opened a door to a threshold that I leapt over with both still-numb feet. If I caused my *own* poor health, did that mean I could also reverse the damage? Could I just tell the MS and optic neuritis to *fuck off*? What if I changed the *shit* instead of waiting around for the *shit* to change on its own?

Since I could take responsibility for my dis-ease, surely I could also take responsibility for healing my dis-ease, and the more I thought about it, the more I embraced the idea. It was just a matter of swapping the narrative.

With that in mind, I got to work.

No lie, I was clueless regarding all the *hows* and *whys*, so I started with the first thing that surfaced for me: victimhood. I told myself, 'Okay, babe, time to lean into responsibility. Let's stop faking who you are and how you feel.' Taking responsibility forced me to stop blaming my mother and father, my DNA, my doctors, my woes, God—even the MS itself—for my situation. Once that happened, I swapped *in* the belief that I could truly participate in my own healing.

To support this new identity, I conjured a vision of what 'healthy' looked like in my present moment. I discarded every negative thought about myself and threw them out. I cleaned up my eating habits. Attended retreats that helped me banish negative emotions, trauma and faulty belief systems I'd been clinging to most of my life. I developed a personal mantra: 'Every day, in every way, I'm getting better and better.' I felt it and said it every morning without fail.

My self-healing journey was, and still is, massive. Swapping out destructive beliefs changed everything about my physical, mental and spiritual health, inspiring and helping me stay open to possibilities. My symptoms lessened once I stopped 'agreeing' to have them, swapping in *only* feelings of health and self-love.

A harder part was contending with all the negative emotions buried inside, all my self-imposed limitations and unconscious beliefs. The sadness. The hurt. The fear, guilt, shame and anger—everything that reinforced my negativity, my desperation to play the victim. Dragging myself out of the dark and into the light got me here ten years later.

Now life looks like this:

- I'm willing to face my past and heal as I go.
- I no longer distrust or shame myself.
- I'm free of addictions and no longer live in hiding.
- I have a profound spiritual connection.
- I'm truly present in life and with others.
- I practise true self-love.
- I no longer suffer from the symptoms I once did.
- I celebrate myself and my achievements, revelling in moments of joy, creativity and gratitude.

Today, I'm an expert in resolving trauma and working with the unconscious self. However, my greatest blessing is helping people around the world embark on their own healing journeys.

And now it's your turn.

I'm So Glad You're Here

Full disclosure: when I first started using the process in this book, I didn't actually know what I was doing. I just knew that *my* symptoms resulted from old trauma and emotional turmoil. I understood that once I'd completely accepted dis-ease into my life, I'd blocked any other thoughts of health and positivity from coming in. Because I thought, felt, talked about and behaved my dis-ease, it's what I became. I was sure of it.

Most importantly, I knew I had to stop the shitshow and swap in something better, because my previous life wasn't a life at all.

It wasn't until years later, while running my own successful coaching business, teaching clients my methods, learning about vibration, studying the sciences of the mind and getting into the vast world of *woo-woo*, that I developed my process into this simple equation: *Stop It, Swap It, Get Present, Take Action* (SSPA).

SSPA became:

- powerful
- immediately effective
- easy to remember
- easy to use anywhere and at any time.

SSPA is designed to interrupt negative thought patterns and promote positive mental states. In this book, I'll show you how to apply it to any life scenario, but particularly to any negative spaces and internal patterns. This book will also help explain why you're here, the true purpose of trauma, hidden factors of the unconscious self and how they all contribute to our eventual need for change. Shaped from actual, factual and lived experiences, it will teach you how to recognise the reasons behind the *whys*—how you tick, why you go through and have been through the things you have. You'll have access to first-hand knowledge and research gleaned from my life, my clients' lives, behavioural science, body science, spirituality and metaphysics.

My method is a blend of science and soul, as they complement each other so perfectly. I've been studying human behaviour for many years; I know it inside and out. Through my experience as a private investigator in England, I gained invaluable knowledge of the nuances of behaviour, body language and interpersonal interactions. This greatly enriched my understanding of the human psyche, allowing me to develop my own powerful processes and training programs, which ultimately led me into the realm of mindset coaching.

I've coached elite athletes, including Olympians, Australian football teams, soccer stars and car racing teams. I've also supported musicians, photographers, directors, parents, and countless families and children in unlocking their potential.

My goal has always been to share what I've learned about why we do what we do, whether with my thousands of individual clients or on stages worldwide. When a client or conference attendee wants to discover their problem, we stare right at it before short-circuiting it and shutting it down for good. Often, that's as simple as applying SSPA. Not only is it applicable at any moment, but it works in mere seconds.

Yes, it's that quick!

My tools work because I continuously test them on myself. My process is thorough. I learn about something, embody it and do it. I reflect on it. Let it soak into me.

Then, I share it.

Then, I *keep* doing it.

I want to acknowledge you for joining me here and stepping out of your comfort zone. Thank you for trusting me and joining me on this life-changing journey. I've got you.

~ Emma

Opportunity In Reinvention

'Don't agree that you have a problem.'

My journey started at the intersection of anxiety, depression, alcoholism and that single profound instruction. What did it mean? How could I not agree to problems I already knew I had? To me, they were inescapable, impacting my life in ways I viewed as entirely permanent.

But back then, I didn't believe I could change anything. I'd lost faith in my ability to create. The mental health diagnoses were stacking up.

Leaving my job and running away had become an hourly contemplation. I'd grown wary of my relationship because I was terrified of getting hurt. The urge to leave Australia and never return was now so intense that it put tears in my eyes. And my poor dog… the twice-daily task of feeding her felt more like a chain binding me to my monotonous routine than an act of loving care. In fact, any minor inconvenience hit me like a sledgehammer to the head.

I'd reached the point where I was over everything. I was done.

Then, I heard it: 'Don't agree that you have a problem.'

Something clicked that day. What would happen if I just decided my problems were no longer problems? That I didn't have to play along anymore? If I tried to change things, would it kill me? Probably not. I wasn't always like this, after all—a fact I'd forgotten over the years—so why couldn't I get back to my old self?

Then, the real penny dropped: Why couldn't I reinvent myself altogether? What was stopping me from reshaping my *entire* way of thinking?

I realised I had a choice at that moment, and I made it. I stopped believing my struggles were immovable truths that I had to accept rather than stories I could rewrite. I stepped beyond the version of myself that couldn't see things any other way.

What I discovered instead was beautiful. That shift in perspective felt like peeking through a door I'd never noticed before. And once I saw the possibilities, I couldn't unsee them.

Here's how my reinvention is going today:

- I no longer have symptoms of depression, anxiety or ADHD.
- I no longer feel the need to drink.
- I no longer despise the gym and foster good health.
- I no longer sabotage relationships or fear trusting people; I'm even married.

- I've regained self-trust and self-belief.
- I can avoid self-shaming when something goes wrong.
- I'm unafraid of facing challenging emotions and old wounds.
- I'm more compassionate; I understand my family and friends better.
- I'm back to creating for myself before others.
- I've started a coaching business and co-authored a book.
- I set aside time for self-care and mindfulness education.
- I feed my soul with experiences and by healing from trauma.

Reinvention is a choice we make when we get tired of all the shit and decide to be brave. Transformation began the moment I stopped agreeing to see permanency in my struggles. Today, I'm not just surviving, but thriving, creating and embracing life with newfound clarity.

And if I can do it, so can anyone else. All it takes is a willingness to step beyond our self-imposed limits and believe we can change—believe that we can SSPA.

~ Bradley

Part One

The Unconscious Sabotage Department

Working Overtime To Keep You Stuck Since Childhood

'Everything you speak is a spell.'
~ Tracy Cecil

'I am my own experiment. I am my own work of art.'
~ Madonna Ciccone

'The first start toward success is to be glad you are yourself.'
~ Florence Scovel Shinn

'Until you make the unconscious conscious,
it will direct your life and you will call it fate.'
~ Carl Jung

'Shame is like everything else; live with it for long enough
and it becomes part of the furniture.'
~ Salman Rushdie

Chapter One

The Illusion of Stuckness

You're Not Trapped, But Your Mind Might Be

Have you been driving through life with the emergency brake on?

Does life feel like you're in a race, and you've got the gas pedal pushed all the way down, but you aren't *really* going anywhere? Can you hear the engine roaring despite your slow-motion crawl? As other cars effortlessly zoom past, are you struck with jealous thoughts? Feelings of frustration?

You, my friend, are not alone.

Many of us go through life battling an internal resistance that keeps us feeling stuck, regardless of the effort we put in. Sure, we chase our dreams, achieve goals and tackle challenges as they show their ugly faces, only to end up spinning our wheels in the same shitty loops of negativity and stress. It's not like we aren't trying, of course, but something deep within us is determined to keep us stationary, refusing to let us continue further down this road we've never travelled.

Luckily, feeling like we're stuck doesn't mean we're *actually* stuck; life isn't a sinister, gruelling race we can't escape. The barriers we experience aren't immovable walls, but more like traffic cones we've left in our own way. And those suckers can be booted the hell off the road.

Feeling stuck can be overwhelming. It's a bloody momentum-killer. It drains our motivation and blocks inspiration. The soul thrives on discovery and growth, and when those go missing, we end up disconnecting from certain parts of ourselves.

Well, this is your cue to pop the metaphorical hood and have a look at what's been wreaking havoc under there. It's time to discover what the problems are, all the things you don't yet know you should look at. You have more control than you think, and trusting in that is the *first* step toward a better driving experience.

That emergency brake isn't locked. It's just waiting for you to release it.

Core Wounds & Misbeliefs

Do negativity & shame run the show?

Negativity is a sneaky bitch. It rarely breaks down the front door and ransacks your life. Instead, it appears as hitting snooze five times because you're still tired, even though you went to bed early. It shows up in your bank account, or the stress you hold in your shoulders. In the look of concern you've started seeing regularly in the mirror. In your heavier-than-usual sighs.

More obvious red flags are when we feel:

- sad
- broke
- unhealthy
- insecure in employment
- mentally or physically pained
- fatigued
- unmotivated
- hopeless.

Are you exhausted after doing absolutely nothing? Does relaxation feel suspicious, or even downright wrong? Does checking your account balance lead to disparaging remarks about yourself? If you can relate to any of this, don't panic! It just means it's time for change. Just because negativity has lingered doesn't mean you have to let it take up residence in your life.

Beliefs & Agreements Holding You Back

Have you ever gone to make toast while you were tired and ended up burning it? Did you lose your shit like I used to? This is a simple but common example of how our unconscious mind can affect us. It's an external overreaction masking internal shame. Our unconscious critic is saying, *Why can't I do something so easy? What's wrong with me? I'm so stupid I can't even make toast.*

I'd blame everything for my burnt toast, even the store, before ever considering that I might've had a case of bad self-belief. I *believed* I was incapable; therefore, it became my reality.

My poor self-belief flared when my teacher announced to my entire class that I was being held back. From that public humiliation, an unconscious agreement formed: *I'm dumb.* Naturally, I shamed the hell out of myself over my failure, so along came another agreement: *I can't.*

BOOM—trauma!

I adopted these negative beliefs:

- 'I can't create.'
- 'I'm not pretty.'
- 'I can't get a good job.'
- 'I'm too much of a mess to manage money and finances.'
- 'I'm far too dumb to write a book.'

These beliefs weren't just fleeting thoughts; they made me feel worse and worse. They became the lens through which I interpreted my reality. Even though they weren't true, to me they *were,* and we become what we believe. The scary thing is that those beliefs could have held me captive forever if I hadn't clued in to my bullshit.

Luckily, I learned to see them for what they *really* were: lies.

Far too often, we come to believe that people are right about us, and that the bad things they say or think are true. When this happens, our unconscious mind stops serving us positively.

However, there's good news: you can throw out belief systems.

Believing You Can't Create

Creating (we aren't just talking art here) is one of the most important things we do in life, hands down. It nourishes our *entire* self, including our soul.

We create in a multitude of different areas:

- change and opportunity
- habits and health
- energy and drive
- love and peace
- wealth and security
- tribes and support systems.

When we assume we lack the ability to create, we put ourselves straight into a state of doubt and resignation. And doubt damages our self-trust. We may second-guess our actions, disengage from opportunities to experiment or explore, and become locked into patterns that don't leave room for anything new. It's not just creation that suffers; the belief narrows our perspective on who we are and what we can achieve. We overlook the inherent creativity already present in how we solve problems, express emotions or adapt to challenges.

When we shift our focus from what we think we lack to what we already have, we prove to ourselves that we can and *have* been achieving. Creativity stops feeling impossible and starts becoming familiar again. By recognising how creativity is embedded in our daily lives, we can then rediscover what we've been capable of all along: change.

Believing You Don't Deserve It

'I don't deserve' traps us in feelings of unworthiness that dictate our actions and choices, often without us realising it. This belief, whether conscious or deeply ingrained in our unconscious mind, influences how we approach relationships, opportunities and self-growth. When we operate under the assumption that we aren't worthy of success, happiness or even love, we make unconscious decisions that reinforce those feelings. It's a loop that sustains itself through avoidance, self-sabotage and settling for less than we truly want or need.

The origin of this belief often lies within the stories we've absorbed about ourselves and our place in the world. These beliefs quietly whisper to us about the things we truly want but feel we can't have, affecting the choices we make and the opportunities we pass up.

When we see worthiness as something inherent rather than earned, we can recognise the limiting beliefs that hold us back. Deserving isn't about entitlement, but reclaiming the right to live fully and authentically.

BE the LIE Forever

The belief systems we have around ourselves are a direct consequence of our thoughts and feelings. That said, we should never feel that we must forever live a lie. We think our beliefs define our *true* identity, but they don't. Feeling 'not good enough' doesn't mean it's true. Being scared doesn't mean we're weak. Thinking we don't belong or that everyone judges us is a lie.

And that's good news! It means if we're thinking it, we can *un-think* it. If we're feeling it, we can *un-feel* it. Beliefs are not facts and, like our thoughts and feelings, can be changed.

Pieces of Your Past Unhealed

Sometimes, our unconscious self believes something that happened in the past is still happening to us today. It isn't true, but we live as though it is because of our ongoing agreements. Good thing we can change them, right? Kishimi and Koga touch on this trauma philosophy:

> *No one experience, in itself, is a cause for our success or failure. We do not suffer from the shock of our experiences—the so-called trauma. Instead, we take from them whatever suits our purpose. Our experiences do not determine us, but the meaning we give them is self-determining. Your life is not something that someone gives you; it's something you choose yourself, and you're the one who decides how you live* (Kishimi & Koga, 2019, p. 12-13).

In other words, trauma doesn't determine what we do with our lives afterwards. We do. Seriously, how different might our lives be if we were taught this in school? But powerlessness has been ingrained in us. We're conditioned to stay wounded and blame, even though it goes against our soul's innate purpose of healing. Our unconscious self says, *Let's hold on to this and pin it to our collar like a badge of honour. It's their fault you're hurt, so wear that like a cloak. It's your protection.*

This blame conditioning works for us about as well as you might expect. It's what keeps us triggered because we'll always respond to our trauma across every aspect of life until we're able to heal from it.

I hate saying that triggers are gifts, but it's true. As counter-intuitive as it sounds, triggers and trauma responses are *actually* good for us. These diagnostic tools show us when we're in agreement with shame. It means there's another layer to uncover within us. There's something else to dig out, and the universe is letting us know. Picture triggers are like the warning lights on a dashboard. When the engine light comes on, it means we need to pull over, look under the hood, figure out what's malfunctioning and fix it. Once that happens, the warning light is no longer needed. Off it goes, and we're back on our way.

What we *don't* want to do is ignore the light and keep driving. The problem in or around the engine won't disappear on its own. It could even affect other mechanical parts, and suddenly we've got a stalled car with the whole dashboard lit up like a Vegas neon sign.

Feelings into Hormones

Although they're often used interchangeably, emotions and feelings differ. Emotions start out as sensations in the body, whereas feelings are generated from our thoughts and influenced by our emotions. Both affect our hormones.

Hormones are the chemical response in the body when we think, feel or experience certain things. While some are good, helping us maintain our mental and physical health, others can be downright nasty, having lasting effects on our unconscious programs and nervous system.

When we experience stress hormones, it means our body thinks we're dealing with something that may be life or death, which is rarely the case. The reality is we've simply had a thought or feeling that triggered a trauma response, and it's caused our body to flood with chemicals. Our heart rates increase, our energy drains and several bodily functions shut down. The real danger here is when we get stuck in a loop of shitty thoughts and feelings because it releases those hormones repeatedly. Over time, stress accumulates, energy levels decline, brain fog thickens and the immune system wears down.

Congratulations! You're now in a perpetual trauma response.

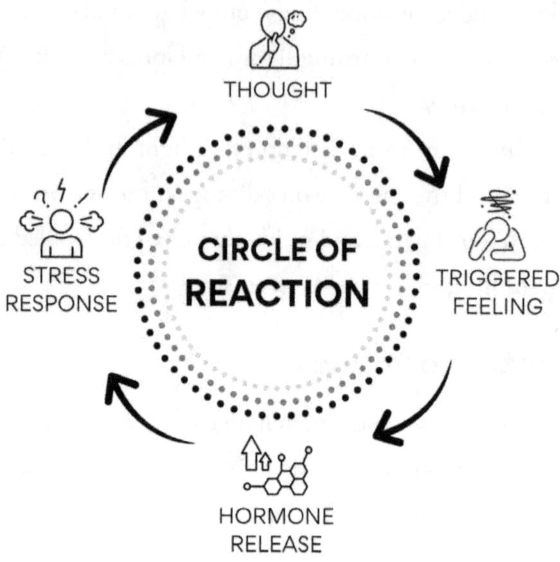

Graphic 1: Circle of Reaction

The Boomerang Effect

Because we can cause the release of hormones simply by thinking and feeling, this opens a door to all kinds of situational triggers. For example, if we evoke an emotional response in someone else, be it a social media post or a triggering conversation, our *own* body reacts as well. The same happens with a friend who shows you a sad video. They evoke sadness in themselves.

In fact, directing feelings and emotions toward other people or things is actually an illusion. Feelings are not outbound, but inbound, always.

Imagine your emotions as a heavy boomerang. When you react, it's like launching a boomerang and expecting it to keep flying to the other side of the field. Instead, it reverses direction and comes right back at you with equal force. When you focus on negativity like judgment, resentment or envy, you may think you've aimed that boomerang toward the metaphorical forest, when *really*, you're setting yourself up to receive a broken nose when it comes rocketing back.

We get caught up in these cycles when we believe our negative feelings can affect another person. The truth is, we aren't affecting them as much as we're affecting ourselves. The negativity we send out into the world doesn't punish the world. It just punishes us and weakens our foundation of self. Holding onto negativity is like holding a heavy stone in your hands, convinced that it's meant for someone else. But in reality, it's only weighing *you* down.

Hormones & Your Gut

Your gut isn't just a tool for intuition and processing food; it's like a second brain (Young, 2012). Packed full of bacteria that help keep us balanced and feeling good, it can reveal a lot about our state of mind and well-being when it gets out of sorts. When we're stressed, anxious or experiencing any number of negative emotions, the release of stress hormones triggers a reaction in the gut. Gut bacteria become disrupted, which can lead to inflammation, illness, irritation, fatigue and other indicators of poor health.

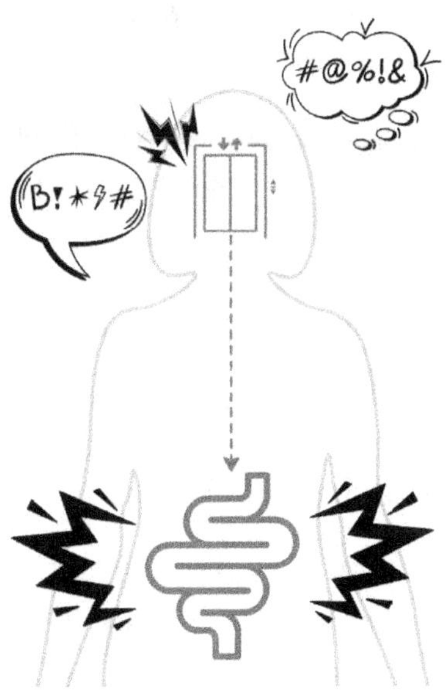

Graphic 2: The Body's Hormone Elevator

Imagine you have an elevator in your head that connects to your gut. Our thoughts use this special elevator. They travel down to the gut, causing us to respond with a feeling. Then, hormones like cortisol and adrenaline are released in response to the feeling. Ultimately, the body responds to those hormones.

I'll be frank: shitty feelings have a stronger impact on us than positive feelings. The corresponding hormones that get released are also more intense, having a drastic effect on our immune system, cells, DNA and energy.

Basically, shit begets shit!

Links to Ageing

A recent study by Kara et al. (2025) found that the gut is linked to the human ageing process, suggesting that negative thoughts and feelings accelerate the ageing process at a cellular level. They weaken and shrink our telomeres, which are the protective caps on our DNA (Brody & Shalev, 2017). Without healthy telomeres, we experience accelerated aging and an increased risk of illness.

Translation: our bodies *literally* wear down from the inside out.

If a thought can make us sick, anxious or sad, it can also make us healthy, happy and good. When we change our thoughts or feelings, we alter the hormones our body releases, giving our body a chance to stop freaking out and our systems a chance to reset. Your gut calms down and your energy returns. It's all about interrupting the cycle.

Neglected or Missing Self-Trust

We're never permanently stuck. We never *can't*. However, we sometimes forget this, resulting in diminished self-trust. 'I can't' is a doozy of an agreement because it signals to our unconscious self the belief that we cannot change course or create something new on our own. We wind up in perpetual victimhood, waiting for a hero to come and rescue us from our own lives. This is a massive abundance-blocker and a belief I struggled to overcome for many years.

We must trust ourselves to change things before we can achieve change. When we don't, we disregard the fact that we actually control the narrative. We fail to see what our built-in diagnostic tools are trying to tell us. Recognising the filters through which we view our world becomes impossible.

Picture yourself wearing a pair of old sunglasses with coloured lenses (or jump to the exercise below). They represent our filters of fear, doubt, shame and unworthiness. What does the world look like through these sunglasses? Do colours appear different or wrong? How about buildings and your surroundings? Are they darker or more sinister than they seemed before? What emotional triggers are you experiencing because of these lenses?

Now imagine taking them off. Reinspect the world around you. What do you see differently without the distortion? I bet things are a lot clearer and correct. When we realise our filters are not us, but rather exaggerations, lies or falsehoods, we regain our power to eliminate them.

To be clear, this isn't about denying the feelings that come with these filters; feelings and emotions are part of being human. It's about not fighting them or proving them true. For example, let's take our most common limiting belief: *I'm not good enough*. It *feels* real when we invest time and effort proving this is true, but it's *not* real. It's just a pair of tinted sunglasses handed to us at some point, which we happily put on and decided never to remove. Eventually, the distortion became so normal that we forgot we were wearing them at all.

But *you* are in charge of *you*, including all your unconscious parts. You *can* change your mind in seconds and stop the bad to swap in for the better, finding self-trust in the present. Pretend you're in an ice cream shop and you've asked for chocolate, but then decide to go with strawberry. See? Mere seconds to change your mind.

The key to embracing self-trust is remembering that you are powerful enough to drive your own story.

You are capable of so much, and *that* is the actual truth.

When we embrace a vision of being better, having better and doing better, our entire self responds in kind. Little hidden belief systems and identities will become more obvious to us. It's not so we feel shame, but so we know what we're working with—allowing us to edit them by stopping, swapping and getting present. Then, everything starts to shift. All those old triggers and wounds won't hurt the way they did before because we'll no longer see them as evidence of our inadequacies. Instead of seeing ourselves through a filter, we'll be able to see ourselves for who *we* truly are.

The next time you have a thought or feeling that doesn't feel good, pause for a moment. Remember that it's not indicative of truth, nor does it cement who you are. Instead, ask yourself what kind of filter you're looking through right now.

This is where the magic begins.

Self-Exploration: What Are My Lenses?

Imagine viewing your life through scratched and strangely tinted sunglasses. Take five to ten minutes and reflect on the following scenarios, using the space provided to journal about or sketch your thoughts.

Through these old sunglasses, my world looks like…

What bothers me most about my surroundings is…

When I remove the sunglasses, my world becomes…

What I love most about my surroundings is now…

Getting the Full Picture?

Everyone exists within the confines of a paradigm. In this context, paradigms refer to a set of assumptions, attitudes, concepts, values, procedures and techniques that form the framework used to interpret the world (Thwaites et al., 2002). They're contextually interchangeable and can both form and skew our perceptions. Mine formed around Catholicism, nature, a tight-knit family unit, a few pinches of small-town conservatism and being the odd one out. They grew powerful, and though I didn't understand what they were or why they existed, I found myself locked in battle with them all the same. Why? Because they didn't allow me to be *me*. They left me feeling as though I was missing something I couldn't explain. The sensation of not doing what I was supposed to in life was often crippling. I knew what I was feeling on a spiritual level, but I didn't know why.

I now know it was my soul trying to remain connected to its purpose, spirit and true self, struggling to stay in touch with *my* reality through *my* paradigms.

However, all I felt was the frustration of living within a framework that I just didn't fit into. No matter which way I changed, I still felt out of place, like someone had handed me a script that didn't belong to my character. What rose from those feelings was self-doubt. It's easy to wonder if you're the problem when you don't fit the role they've told you to play.

But the issue isn't you. It's the cultural and mental paradigm that's shaped your perception of what's supposed to be. The way we perceive ourselves and our norms plays a massive role in how positively or negatively we experience life. It's important to remember that what we think of ourselves and who we *truly* are, are two very different things. So many of us accept our self-perception as fact, not realising it's often just a reflection of the environment we grew up in.

Here's some promising news: since external influences shape our paradigms, we can reshape these paradigms as we discover the ones that don't fit. And once we recognise *that* possibility, our entire world opens up.

- Bradley

Chapter Two

A Higher-Quality Life

Time To Fire Negativity & Hire Abundance

It's amazing what can happen when we let go of negativity. Life doesn't just get lighter, it gets easier. We get to reclaim clarity of thought and make informed decisions. The impossible no longer feels out of reach.

How different would your day be without stress and self-doubt weighing it down? Would your relationships be stronger? I think so. How about a more rewarding career? You bet. And self-confidence? Unshakeable. When negativity no longer wields power over your moods and choices, power returns to you. You regain your ability to move forward with purpose.

Mind you, launching into a state of toxic positivity isn't the aim, either.

So, what does it take to ditch negativity for good? It starts with practising the switch between recognising when negativity sneaks in and shutting it down before it overtakes us.

It begins with practical strategies to:

- prevent automatic negative thoughts and emotions
- switch to or maintain a positive mindset
- live in the present instead of the past or future
- actively build healthier, more confident habits.

In other words, it starts with SSPA.

Negativity & Stress

What are the five biggest areas of life affected?

Health

Negativity isn't just a mood; it messes with your health. Think spiking cortisol levels, a weakened immune system, headaches, digestion issues and chronic sleep disturbances. A troubled or heavy state of mind wipes your energy levels and increases your chances of becoming sick.

When we swap our way out of negativity, our mind and body respond to the shift. We usually sleep better, overcome exhaustion and have more energy, make healthier choices and reduce our cravings for coping mechanisms like alcohol and junk food. These changes can then ripple through other parts of life.

Wealth

Believe it or not, your state of mind has a direct influence on your financial situation, as do your agreements regarding money. Negativity can lead to a scarcity mindset. This restricts many opportunities, leading you to view success and financial growth as unattainable. You may grow unsure of your future security, or even believe you'll never have enough to be happy.

It isn't true, so *fuck* that right off.

Rising from that kind of mindset replaces fear with confidence, meaning we're more willing to notice random opportunities as they come into our space, or take smart risks we'd otherwise avoid. Wealth isn't just about money. It's believing in your ability to create abundance and a solid financial standing.

Now that *is* true.

Career

Do you live in a cycle of hesitation and self-doubt? Are you constantly second-guessing your abilities and backing away from challenges? It's the influence of factors such as negativity, fear and unconscious shame. Instead of seeing possibilities, we often end up focusing on what could go wrong.

Stepping away from negativity means our careers benefit in powerful ways: stronger performances, better work relationships and unexpected recognition. Workplaces usually reward confidence and resilience, so break up with negativity and reclaim both.

Relationships

Negativity can poison relationships by making us defensive, unfair or withdrawn. It affects how we communicate and connect with others, especially when we're under stress or always expecting the worst.

Our relationships bloom when we distance ourselves from negativity and stress. It allows us to be better listeners, practise patience and become more understanding of our partners, family and friends. We respond with trust and empathy rather than scepticism and a cold shoulder. Our connections grow deeper because they're built on positivity and genuineness.

Self-Confidence

You might not have considered this as worthy of the top five list, but I assure you it belongs here. That's because without it, we can become convinced we aren't good enough, smart enough or capable enough to manage the other areas of life well.

That's negativity at its core: a confidence thief.

So, give it the big old boot.

When we stop letting negativity run the show, we discover that confidence isn't about never failing. It's about not letting our failures define us, so we can start to see ourselves in a different light. Our confidence comes back. We believe in our ability to handle life's challenges. Unlocking a bolder, fully capable version of ourselves helps us chase the life we deserve.

From the Case Files: Money Judgement

Once upon a time, a good friend of mine believed that if she became financially successful, her family would stop speaking to her.

This belief formed during her childhood and was reinforced as she grew by a family that disparaged wealth. She developed an identity of unworthiness associated with having money. Money became something not to acquire or use, so she always struggled to manage it: it went out as quickly as it came in.

On a recent visit home, she discovered this unconscious identity of hers. She quickly realised where it originated and how it had been running her financial show.

Sitting with her family on the front porch, overlooking the river, surrounded by freshly renovated holiday homes, the familiar shit-talk started.

'Imagine how much he spent on that jet ski… they just got back from Europe… what idiots, wasting all that money… look at these two new units going up over here… look at the owners, they think they're so great…'

As my friend listened, her unconscious programming came to light: basics are enough, and anything more is shameful. To want nice things meant her family would reject her.

That was the day everything changed.

Now, mismanaging money is a distant memory. And I am so *fucking* proud of her.

Your Body: A Trauma 'Rubbish Dump'

What's piling up & where is it hidden?

Many people don't realise that illness can be triggered by trauma. It's an unconscious reaction and, therefore, easily overlooked. This is a reality we must face without self-blame or self-shame because we have no control over how our trauma will manifest, and punishing ourselves only makes things worse.

In April 2013, I nearly became a paraplegic when I tore every ligament in my neck in a roller skating accident. The recovery alone took three months, during which I had the chance to reflect on some truths I'd been burying for decades. *Had* the chance… but didn't do it. Instead, I remained in avoidance.

It was April the following year that I went blind in my left eye and received my swath of diagnoses.

Still, I ignored it. 'I'm just ill,' I'd say. 'It is what it is. Nothing's causing this to happen to me.'

It took three months of getting sicker and sadder and less independent before I accepted that there was something more I needed to look at: that unhealed trauma can trigger dis-ease. As I began to heal, I realised I'd been blind because I was full of anger. I was *literally* blind with rage.

Most people assume that when they begin to feel the same pain they experienced at a moment of trauma, the healing process isn't working. It actually works the other way around, and that's so important to remember. When we don't allow ourselves to go through pain to reach a breakthrough, we stay in the cycle of trauma, forced to relive it again and again.

There are three stages to the cycle of trauma:

- acute stage
- suppression stage
- chronic stage.

Acute Stage

The acute phase features raw, sensory trauma from a painful or overwhelming event. Due to societal conditioning, our response to this acute discomfort is to suck it up and move on. Rather than process the event, we push it deep down to avoid the pain.

Suppression Stage

In the suppressed stage, we ignore the trauma and think we've dealt with it well enough. Unconsciously, however, it lingers.

Chronic Stage

Over time, the trauma becomes 'chronic.' At this point, it has sunk so far down that we're no longer aware of it, yet it manifests in various ways: in physicality, mentality, emotion and spirituality, with unfavourable effects.

To overcome trauma, it needs to be released in the reverse order.

As chronic trauma resurfaces, it first moves into the suppressed stage and then back into the acute stage. Once it's at the surface again, it's ready to be processed and healed.

However, most people stop here. When they feel pain associated with the trauma, they think continuing the process will be too hard, or that it won't work. Therefore, they suppress their trauma once more, causing it to recede back down and retake the chronic form.

So, the cycle continues.

How does the body cope with this? What happens when we repeatedly shove trauma back down and allow it to fester?

The short answer is that it gets stored somewhere *in* the body. It affects our lymphatic system and the vagus nerve, a long cranial nerve that plays a significant role in the parasympathetic nervous system. *The Body Keeps the Score: Brain, Mind, and Body in the Healing of Trauma,* by renowned psychiatrist Kolk (2014), explains that trauma isn't just a psychological issue, but also *physiological.* When a person experiences traumatic events such as abuse, violence or war, the brain's normal functioning can be disrupted, affecting how the individual processes emotions, memories and stress. These disruptions can lead to a wide range of symptoms, including anxiety, depression, flashbacks, dissociation and more.

In short, the body physically reacts to trauma.

Many of my clients reported a reduction or total disappearance of a health issue after releasing trauma. Their experiences illustrate how the body, mind and energy are tightly intertwined.

By avoiding thoughts and feelings triggered by our trauma, we wind up holding them in the body and mind. We must allow ourselves to feel and release at *each* stage, even when it feels tough. Only then does true healing occur.

The good news is that the pain of healing rarely lasts long. But avoidance will make that shit last forever. That pain lasts all day, every day, my friend.

Negativity Comes in Bundles

What bad energy 'add-ons' are you investing in?

Because of energy, vibration and magnetism, 'lack' rarely shows up solo. When we hold negative beliefs, they create an energetic agreement that attracts more negativity, as we're vibrating on the same frequency. If there's anything I can't stress enough, it's that agreements *are* a vibrational package deal.

If you agree that you're struggling with money or wealth, the universe will then say, 'I hear you loud and clear… so, here you go!' It will give you more struggle. Suddenly, you won't just be struggling with money. You'll be struggling with everything.

I know what you're thinking: You just wouldn't be in agreement with that, right? Perhaps not, but what you would be in agreement with is the *doubt*. How bloody frustrating is that? It's *all* energy, so be careful what kind you're signing up for!

Your Energy, Your Life

What's the hidden impact of vibration?

Florence Shinn produced my favourite frequency quote in her book *The Magic Path of Intuition* when she wrote, 'A harmonious person is never vibrating at the same rate as a germ' (Shinn, 2013, p. 236). It's just so on point because humans *do* vibrate, and we *are* meant to at a higher level. In fact, all matter and energy exist in a matching frequency. Vibration is a byproduct of what we think, feel and agree about ourselves, affecting the energy we put into the world.

We also magnetise energy toward us. More importantly, this energy will ultimately align with our *current* vibrational level. A life filled with high-frequency emotions, like love and joy, naturally attracts positive energy.

But it works the other way around as well. When we sit in a state of hatred, emptiness, illness, scarcity, poverty or shame, we draw in more of these low-vibration experiences. Agreements are a package deal, remember? If we have deep shame, we open ourselves up to attract *all* the other bottom-rung things as well. That is *not* where we want to be if we're looking for a satisfying life!

Do you have many accidents? Are any pretty major? Are you struggling to achieve? Do you get bullied? Unconsciously, you could be affecting your vibrational level by being in agreement with shame. Low-vibrational things hold much more mass compared to those at high vibrations, which is why it can be such a challenge to pull away from them and strive for a better life. This is the hidden fuckery of our unconscious self and its default operating mode. *Everything's hard. Everything's difficult.* When we invest energy in feeling broken, sick or 'not enough', it becomes the foundation of our future.

That's when life gets extra shitty. We find ourselves under massive amounts of pressure, weighed down, depressed, chronically fatigued and, as so many of my clients have described, like we're living at the bottom of a well with no way of climbing out.

But we *must* find footholds. The secret lies in the relative weight of the items at the top of the pyramid compared to those at the bottom. We need more of *all* the positive things we do for ourselves and those around us in order to outweigh the negative.

Time to start the climb!

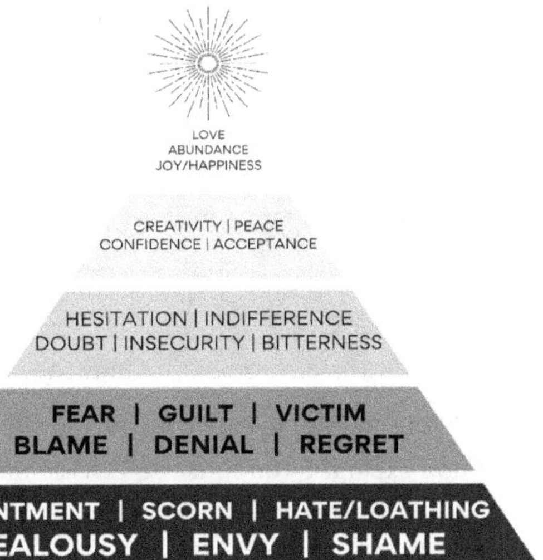

Graphic 3: The Pyramid (Weight)

The Eagle & The Pine

I'm a free-spirited forest girl, and nature is where I really thrive.

So come to the forest with me.

Imagine the gamut of your energetic states as a massive pine tree. This tree is ancient, sturdy and healthy, slowly growing whether you notice or not.

And you? You're the eagle choosing what you observe around and beyond the tree, which branches you regularly circle and, most importantly, where you perch.

The tree's lowest branches are pure survival. Down here, it's cold. Light hardly reaches you or the forest floor. Surrounding you is decay, frost and shadows. The awareness of danger continually preoccupies your thoughts and senses. Down here, you're sitting at your lowest vibrational level.

On these branches, your vision is limited to the short range of what's directly in front of you. Your nervous system is in continuous protection mode, meaning your current choices are made based on finding safety from threats. You've become highly skilled at surviving, but it isn't the same as living or thriving.

In fact, merely surviving is your *only* real option. You can't see any other way amongst the underbrush and neighbouring trees.

So you brace for pain and disappointment. You cope. You endure. You numb out when it all gets too hard. Since your body is constantly bracing itself for threats, there's no opportunity for growth, because you cannot heal in survival mode.

It's high time to get out of there!

As you take off and rise through the branches of this ancient pine, your situation begins to change. The air warms, the light gets stronger and your range of vision expands. You find you can see more than just threats and ways to survive. Above the shadows, the world is full of patterns. Possibilities. Thermals that you can ride even higher. Every branch upward provides more clarity and less confusion. More *responding* and less reacting. More wisdom, ease and love. More effective healing techniques. Higher vibrational levels.

You reach the treetop.

This is where the eagle *belongs*.

From the pine tree's crown, you can see the whole landscape: forests, rivers, weather systems and the very movement of life itself. Nothing here is personal, urgent, uncomfortable, shitty or scary. Up here, you have endless sight and the best options for your life. Everything makes sense away from what dwells at ground level. This is where your soul naturally operates. You're *designed* for the treetops because freedom thrives where fear cannot. You've finally found true peace, abundance and light.

SSPA is how we stop clinging to the pine bark and start trusting our wings. It's how we move from branch to branch. Solving our problems requires us to climb that tree and expand our awareness. Otherwise, we'll only find low-value solutions that keep us in low vibrational levels, operating in survival mode and always under perceived threat. Elevating means acting in higher-value ways because we can *see* high-value options that were invisible to us before.

That said, we all elevate in our own time. We don't have to scale the whole tree in one day. We only need to rise one branch higher than where we currently are.

And as we do, our lowest state also rises. With enough consistent elevation, our 'bottom' branch becomes one at mid-tree instead of the ground. In fact, we may hardly recognise what once felt like our default survival state, because the shadows no longer feel like a place we'd ever choose to perch again.

I refuse to live on the lowest branches these days. I no longer 'perch' in the vibrations that bring me down, because they don't align with the life I now maintain.

And it's staying that way.

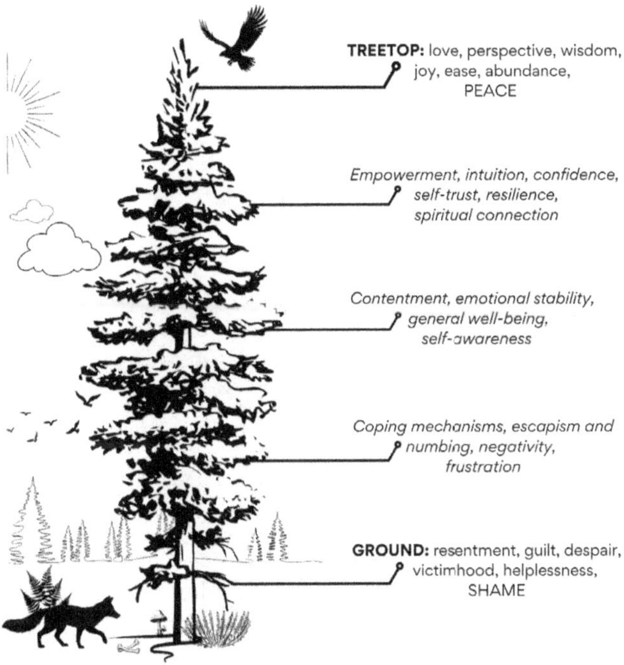

Graphic 4: The Awareness Scale

Self-Exploration: What If...

Take a few minutes to journal about these potent questions. Ponder the possibilities and think limitlessly.

What if my life didn't include negativity, stress and frustration?

What if I believed in something different?

What if I viewed myself through a filter of compassion, trust and possibility?

Negativity's Effect on Momentum

Imagine you're on a travelator at an airport, and at the end of this moving walkway is the version of yourself you aspire to be. The travelator glides you forward effortlessly toward the *new* you. You're excited, moving unhindered in the direction you wish to go.

Then, the thoughts come: *I'll be that happy when I lose weight… I don't deserve to be that person… I'm not yet good enough.*

The belt jerks and then slows to a crawl.

Feelings of frustration and anxiety overtake you because you're no longer moving quickly and effortlessly toward the new you. In fact, you aren't *really* moving toward anything at all.

You yell at the travelator, demanding it speed up again, then shame yourself for getting on that thing in the first place. 'See? I'm not good enough to get where I need to go,' you say, loud enough to turn heads. 'I'm useless.'

The travelator's motor grinds the belt to a halt. A cloud of smoke rises as the belt shudders, then reverses direction—the potential of a new you retreats. The belt takes you further and further back. You rage against the ground you've lost, resentful and seething, desperate to go back the other way, back toward the new you, hating yourself for being lazy, for not just walking. But the more you fight, the faster you're dragged back, and the more exhausted you grow.

Eventually, you stop. *Why am I struggling so much? There wasn't a problem before I started tearing myself down. Maybe* I'm *the one stopping my forward momentum.*

The smoke clears.

You look back at the new you, waving, beckoning you forward.

With a deep breath, you sit down. You calm your mind, wrap yourself in a bear hug and speak lines of self-appreciation. The belt screeches to a halt, then moves forward once again; all resistance is gone as the travelator picks up speed. You're back in a glide, heading toward the *new* you, all smiles and love.

And this time, you understand: your progress isn't hastened by force, fights or punishment. Travelling with ease requires trust and surrender—self-compassion over self-condemnation. You see how every harsh reaction did nothing but slow you down.

So, you let go. You choose to embrace the journey and continue to move forward.

And this time, it's for good.

~ Bradley

Chapter Three

Meet Your Five Selves

They've Seen Some Things

Countless frameworks land on the same truth from their own unique angles. But it was only after working with my friend Jason Parks, an energetic therapy specialist, that I understood to my *core* that we are multi-dimensional beings. We're layered, intelligent and exquisitely designed by a higher power. And each aspect of *us* plays a crucial role in our existence, including how we perceive the world, interact with others and navigate our internal programs.

An important part of healing is learning how our different parts communicate, protect and guide us.

So let's get metaphysical.

The Spirit, The Source

Knowledge, information, impartiality

At our core, our spirit is the seed of light that connects us to the source of all creation. It represents unlimited potential and provides our inspiration. Essentially, our spirit *is* Source experiencing itself through human form.

While infinite, it cannot taste, touch or feel in the ways we do. It's an observer, which means it rarely intervenes in the process of life.

To gather data and understanding, our spirit enters an energetic 'contract' with our soul. Through this soul contract, it undertakes the human journey, collecting data, knowledge and experiences that contribute to the ever-expanding nature of creation itself.

Source is also referred to as the higher self, the Creator, God or a number of other things. It's not simply the universe but something far greater. In fact, the universe itself is a creation of this infinite force, as are the universes both within and beyond ours.

Source is not male or female, nor a figure with a white beard, and certainly not bound to or defined by religion. It's pure creative potential—limitless, eternal and beyond human understanding. It's the essence of *literally* everything; the source from which all things emerge.

The Soul

Impulse, experience, elevation

Our soul is ancient, having existed for millions of lifetimes, travelling through different planets, dimensions and universes. It carries the wisdom, wounds and countless experiences from our earthly journeys, but it's always eager for more. Through the creation of experiences, like warmth, beauty, abundance and connection, our soul seeks fulfilment and healing.

Spirit and Soul work in harmony. Our spirit seeks knowledge and expansion, while our soul, driven by experience and growth, is the active traveller. It thrives *outside* of its comfort zone, searching for purpose under the contract it made before entering this physical realm.

Imagine our spirit reaches out: 'Hey, Soul. I need data, and I need it from Earth.' Just as it has with souls from other realms (Andromeda, other galaxies and even other realities), this time, the focus is on a *human* life.

Soul says, 'Sure, what kind?'

Spirit might say, 'I want to understand resilience. How much can the human spirit endure before it breaks? And more importantly, how can it rise again? How can it transform suffering into love and be better than before?'

'Sounds like an intriguing challenge. Let's do it.'

Or perhaps Spirit says, 'I want to understand the depths of forgiveness.'

To which Soul happily replies, 'No problem. We'll make that a theme for this lifetime.'

The Lost Art of Soul Purpose

Western culture has grown almost obsessed with the idea of finding one's purpose, but we often go wrong when we don't understand that life's purpose is not the same as our *soul's* purpose. When I refer to Soul's purpose, I'm not talking about that book you want to write or the desire to be onstage in front of an audience. It doesn't mean a career. Fulfilling though they may be, these are simply goals checked off along life's path.

Our soul's true purpose is to heal, elevate and experience.

When we seek life's purpose and not Soul's purpose, we wind up heading in directions that don't sustain or fulfil us, feeling stuck after coming to dead ends or reinforcing negative patterns and limiting beliefs.

In healing, we make room for our goals to align with our intentions. We create space to take action, and our soul takes advantage of this by putting ideas in our heads that will help us evolve.

When we set out on an inspired path, we can help ourselves along by asking a crucial question: 'Which parts of me do I need to heal so they can align with my goal?'

For example, if I want to start a business, I want to heal the parts of me that view my business goal as difficult or impossible. When we view something as unachievable, it means we aren't quite in alignment with it. We know when our soul has healed because our goals feel normal instead of hard.

By considering goals and aspirations as our life's purpose, we prevent ourselves from seeing beyond that moment of creation in the universe. What I mean is, what happens once we've achieved our goal? If you perceive your purpose as writing a book, what happens when you finish that book? If you've done the most important thing you thought you would, does your life become meaningless?

Absolutely not. It means your soul is ready for its next adventure.

Our soul is driven by improvement and experience. It wants to play. It wants to travel. It wants to fall in love and make love and give love. Cry. See art. Feel moved. Connect with nature. Dance. It loves music. It craves the healing and abundant energies of Spirit. It wants to give back. It wants to live. But it needs one more thing to make this happen: a vehicle.

And so Soul steps into its temporary vessel—its corporeal form.

The Physical Body

Response, sensation, activity

Our physical form is how the soul interacts with the material world. This body is nothing more than an outfit that allows us to touch, hold, taste and move through life with *all* the sensations humans experience.

Our body isn't random either. It's purpose-built, tailored for the Soul during this lifetime. No matter its shape, size or uniqueness, it's *exactly* as it needs to be and reflects our soul's chosen journey.

It's important to remember that this body is not who we are, but merely the tool by which we experience.

Cellular Memory

Every year, science is increasingly proving that every cell in our body holds memory. The body contains about thirty-eight trillion cells, which climbs to seventy trillion if you include the body's elaborate bacteria, and each one holds a strand of DNA (Sender et al., 2016).

Every single cell has a micro-influence on our unconscious memory and behavioural programs. So from birth to death, our cells carry and store patterns, experiences and beliefs. However, our cells are constantly dying and renewing, which means biologically speaking, we're capable of complete renewal in a relatively short amount of time. Brain excluded, every bone, organ and component of our body regenerates within a few weeks to a few years (Fausto et al., 1989; Parmacek & Epstein, 2009; Pearce et al., 2017).

So why then do our struggles, pains and chronic conditions persist?

Because we have an identity around them, the body listens to what *we* focus on. Our cells remember our repeated feelings and emotional responses. If we're suffering from pain or disease, our words and thoughts can *literally* reinforce it.

The key is to change the agreement. Stop feeding yourself the same limiting narrative and swap out those destructive thoughts. Our bodies aren't keeping us stuck. *We* are. It's why agreements are so important.

But when you abandon a long-held identity and belief, who remains? To help us navigate all of this, we need another self to get in the game.

Our Consciousness

Thought, logic, choice

We aren't *just* passengers in our own bodies, but creators of our *own* experience. Our consciousness allows us to operate with autonomy and awareness. It's the exploratory aspect of ourselves, capable of understanding complex concepts beyond our senses, space and time (Lycan, 1995).

With a predetermined life path, experience would be irrelevant, wouldn't it? No need to gather new data. What makes life meaningful is having the ability to *choose* our way forward. We aren't powerless, and we can decide how we respond.

Our consciousness is critical for rewriting our story and stepping into new identities. Suffering should be a *temporary* breakdown that leads us to create something new in its wake.

Forty Bits of Information

We receive fragments of sensory information from our surroundings every second, on the order of millions to one billion (Ardalan, 2024; Ware, 2025), which is an astonishing amount of data available to process in real time. Consciously, the brain can only take in a microscopic fraction of data. In the 1990s, before the internet and smartphones, Csikszentmihalyi and Nakamura (2010) estimated the number to be around 120-160 bits. However, a study by Zheng et al. (2024) found that the number had since reduced, even suggesting that it is now as terrifyingly low as ten.

What's more, these ten to forty bits will differ from me to you. Sure, we may have some overlap, but the majority of data will depend on who we are at that moment.

The information our brain processes is determined by our:

- mood/mindset
- beliefs/identity
- values
- environment
- unconscious programming.

Therefore, with the help of our unconscious self, the brain will delete, distort and generalise the information it deciphers from the ten to forty bits it takes in. It means we're back to seeing ourselves and others through a filter.

Seriously brain?

As if understanding the full picture wasn't challenging enough, the added sabotage only makes it harder.

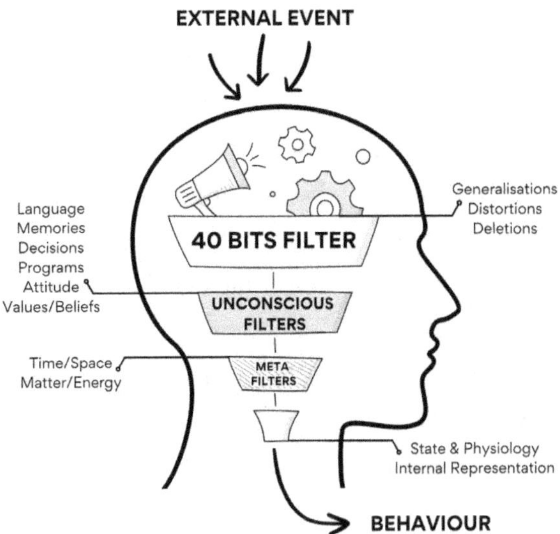

Graphic 5: Structure of Reality

Let's go back to those sunglasses with different coloured lenses for a second.

Put them on and consider the following scenarios:

1. Mike believes that all dogs are dangerous. So, when he walks past a park and sees two dogs playing, his brain filters this down to mean they're attacking each other violently. This distortion is Mike's truth, even though it isn't reality.

2. Sarah struggles with feelings of inadequacy. A friend calls her and says, 'Thanks for helping me today. You're just awesome!' Because of her filters, Sarah concludes her friend is being facetious. Although her interpretation isn't accurate, to her it *is*, and her self-doubt increases as a result.

3. Kate and Ben are speaking with Melanie, a baker with two kids, at a party she's throwing. On the drive home, Kate says to Ben, 'How lovely were Melanie's cakes?' Ben didn't see any cakes there, but Kate described them sitting on the snack table. Because Ben doesn't like cake, his brain deleted those fragments of 'cake'

information from his awareness. To him, there were no cakes at all. Later on, Kate mentions Melanie's husband. Ben says, 'She doesn't have a husband. She has two teenage boys.' Kate swears she heard something about a husband, not realising her brain had generalised the situation based on her perception of what a family unit should look like.

4. Sam is in a real mood. Over coffee with a friend, they shit-talk and gossip about people. Then, Sam gets a text from their partner: *Hey, hope you're having a nice coffee.* Because of their mood and environment, they filter this down to sarcasm and feel disrespected. 'Wow, he doesn't think I have anything better to do than get coffee? What a dickhead.' The next day, Sam's mood had changed. They still meet with their friend, but this time their conversation is warm and peaceful. Sam receives the same message from their partner: *Hey, hope you're having a nice coffee.* Today, Sam filters bits of information that match their positive mood and environment. 'Aw, he's thinking of me. I love him.'

Situations like this happen constantly. We tend to focus on what aligns with our inner state and ignore or alter the rest. Many of my clients do the same, trapped in the same old negative spaces. *School was crap… My partner's a jerk… Nothing ever works out.*

Stopping and swapping helps them shift their focus away from these old beliefs and onto empowerment, growth and possibilities. Everyone is one hundred per cent right, but only for themselves. Our perception of reality shapes *our* reality, and once we recognise this, seeing the bigger picture becomes easier. Then, instead of identifying ourselves by our filters, we can use them as a tool to see what needs to be tweaked, thrown out or changed.

Which leads us to our last self.

The Communicator Body

Contrast, correspondence, triggers

Why spend time guessing, dissecting or overanalysing when we already have an internal system giving us the feedback we need? Instead of seeking answers externally, we can listen to the innate intelligence within us, which I now call the communicator body.

The five-selves model I learned from Jason Parks includes a part of us often referred to as the *pain body*. It's a rightly named self because it comprises our pain, triggers, discomforts and dis-ease—a 'bag of trauma', as Jason once put it. In a nutshell, it remembers our unresolved wounds.

Wounding aside, our fifth self is highly intelligent and deeply compassionate, and the *purpose* it drives is critical for our growth. When we get used to reading its signals, we can interact with it from an elevated perspective. Seeing past the pain, we notice that its goal is to communicate with us: getting our attention, highlighting misalignments and showing us where things need care or safety for our soul to heal.

This is trauma-informed guidance at its finest, and it doesn't exist to truly hurt us.

Yes, it stores our unresolved emotional experiences, personal wounding, ancestral trauma and unconscious programs, but for the purpose of *alerting* us to their existence. It recalls what we have yet to integrate, process, move on from, heal, forgive, understand or otherwise overcome. This can include old stories we've let define us over time, memories we can't release and belief systems that negatively impact our well-being.

The communicator body speaks to us through:

- triggers
- emotional charge
- anxiety
- physical pain

- repeating patterns
- sudden or dramatic reactivity.

When we understand the true reason for our communicator body, it becomes one of the most powerful diagnostic tools we possess. It points us directly to our growth opportunities.

The problem? We don't use it for its intended purpose. Instead, we numb it out. From childhood, it's how we've been taught to relate to discomfort. We're conditioned to avoid anything that feels unpleasant. *Don't look there… Don't open that door… Don't feel that.*

Instead of listening, we drown out or suppress the unpleasant feelings with coping mechanisms, leading us into long-term habits that deactivate our senses.

These coping mechanisms can be:

- alcohol
- food
- porn
- distraction
- overworking
- endless scrolling
- unnecessary medication
- self-isolation.

When we ignore our communicator body, unresolved issues remain stored within us. While our soul craves the opportunity to heal, our communicator body adapts to our coping mechanisms, creating stagnation wrongly coded as safety. Over time, this disconnects us from our other selves, leaving us feeling flat, unmotivated and lacking purpose. The nervous system just wants to settle, and if numbing worked before, the communicator body will choose it again. Until we stop identifying with our discomfort, choose to listen openly and heal, *stuck* is where we'll stay.

But we aren't broken, and we certainly aren't *meant* to live in discomfort.

Learning to recognise the messages as they come to us can mean the difference between feeling relentlessly attacked and like we're receiving a gentle knock on the metaphorical door. Instead of hearing the message, 'Something is wrong with you,' we can start to listen differently. 'Hey, you're being hard on yourself again. You've drifted into a story that's unkind or untrue. Come back to self. To love.'

The relationship I had with my communicator body changed when I changed the name. My clients relaxed more, listening instead of bracing. The work we did became more graceful and less jarring; more collaborative, and with less resistance.

So the next time you feel a twinge of discomfort, listen *inward* for the answer. Where might you need to give yourself some extra love? Where in life do you feel you're missing safety? What signals are you receiving? Where is your communicator body asking to be heard?

We *must* shift our relationship with it and start observing it as a guide or compass pointing to where we're getting in our own way. Every trigger is information, every action a map designed by our inner messenger. Then, once we've stopped seeing the signals as pain and discomfort to alleviate, we recognise them as quicker pathways to awareness, alignment and healing.

'Doctor Gabriel'

I call my communicator body *Gabriel* because it's the archetype of divine communication. This isn't mysticism so much as a symbol of clear and neutral messaging, communicating what my system is holding onto and what my soul is ready to resolve and release.

Imagine Gabriel as an inner diagnostic doctor who reads the body, emotions and energy field, then provides us with a precise report. It shows us where we're misaligned with what our soul needs.

Understanding how to read this 'report' is especially important when we look at chronic pain, illness or repeated injuries. They aren't random, nor are they meaningless. Pain is information, and one of the most articulate languages of our communicator body.

Long-term pain is often the body alerting us to:

- something unresolved
- something being carried alone
- something not yet felt or processed through
- something that makes us feel unsafe
- a damaging behaviour or coping mechanism.

I frequently reference works by Evette Rose when supporting clients with chronic issues. Her metaphysical models show how specific physical symptoms tie to different emotional and energetic conflicts within us (Rose, 2013). Her work beautifully aligns with the communicator body and reinforces the idea that our body isn't malfunctioning, but *expressing*.

It means someone with pain in their left knee should be treated both physically *and* energetically. Just like our feelings and triggers, the communicator body uses sensation as a correspondence pathway. Think tightness, inflammation, exhaustion, repetition, injury and, of course, pain. These are the diagnostics of a highly intelligent doctor who's saying, 'This is where attention is needed.'

It's important to note the difference between understanding the message and bringing it onboard as part of our identity, because the message *isn't* who we are. It's simply an indicator that we have something to work on.

I once worked with a young cricketer who was being drafted for the Australian cricket team. He'd experienced repeated concussions from accidents, missteps and strangely timed events, none of which related to gameplay. These concussions *looked* physical on the surface, but his communicator body, his Gabriel, had been alerting him to something much deeper: a fear of success. Becoming the person he'd always dreamt of being felt unsafe to his nervous system. The expected visibility felt dangerous; the responsibility seemed overwhelming. For his system, such expansion was a threat. So the communicator body intervened, slowing his career until his system felt safe enough to receive what he wanted. In other words, preparation for success.

But Gabriel was also revealing a misalignment between his self-perception and *true* self. The cricketer's injuries were signals: *what you're thinking up here isn't who you are.*

Sometimes Gabriel's communication can be awfully fucking dramatic. My coping mechanism of choice used to be alcohol, which I used to mentally numb myself for years. So when my communicator body had had enough of me not listening to its subtler signals, it *physically* numbed me.

First it was my feet, and then my hands.

After that, a whole leg.

It took out half of my body before I finally said, 'Shit, I've been ignoring something here.'

This is the power of our fifth self. What can often look like dis-ease, pain, sabotage or blocks is actually a protective measure enacted while we prepare for expansion. The beauty of this system is that chronic pain becomes a type of dialogue once we understand it's not an enemy. Then instead of fighting symptoms, we use them to change our behaviour and elevate.

Gabriel is here to help us grow with honesty. And when we learn to listen, we can heal with grace rather than failing under our own force. Integrating and balancing the five aspects of Self is a complex part of our human nature, but by working with each part and gaining a better understanding of their roles, it becomes easier to heal and grow. We live more harmoniously within ourselves and the world, loving more, elevating more and building toward our highest potential.

We are truly amazing beings.

Self-Exploration: My Communicator Body

Take five to ten minutes to reflect on where you think your communicator body is in control. Journal or sketch on the following questions.

NB: If you need help, join our Stop It Swap It - Official Readers Group www.facebook.com/groups/stopitswapit.

Remember that this is not about self-shaming, but realisation and awareness. Do this somewhere that isn't the couch or bed; standing or walking around will give the best results. The more fearful you are of writing it down, the more important it is that you do.

The fear is your communicator body saying, 'This is where we need to look. It's an opportunity to release and grow.'

So go *there*, I urge you. This book is the safest space you'll ever have to start doing the work, free from consequence and judgement.

Remember, I've got you!

Communicator body:

How am I behaving?

Who or what is affected?

What are the consequences?

What does this list reveal about me when my triggers, pain or fear are in control?

How old am I when I'm not the one in control?

Which 'me' is motivating my communicator body?

Unconscious Dirt, Conscious Cleanliness

It's shocking to me that only forty fragments of information make it into our consciousness every second, considering the mammoth amount we're unconsciously absorbing all the time. But it's true: our unconscious mind is aware of an ocean of data our conscious mind isn't.

Think back to the last time you stepped into a friend's home. Did you notice any dusty areas they missed when they last cleaned? Maybe a wayward throw pillow? Spot any faded stains on the carpet or worn edges on the staircase? Could you see remnants of ash around the fireplace?

Did your friend seem oblivious?

Don't worry, you aren't obsessive-compulsive.

You were just taking in new information, data that your friend had already processed and stored away in their unconscious mind. Their familiar environment has faded into the background of their awareness.

This is the reality of unconscious information processing. It means we often aren't aware of 'dirt' in our house until it's gone. Our unconscious self registers the data, but *we* don't. Instead, we distort, delete or generalise it away.

Now, what do you think would happen if you cleaned up those very minor problem areas in your friend's home without telling them? Would they notice the change?

You bet they would.

It's not until something improves, even in the subtlest ways, that we notice the difference. When data changes, it must be reprocessed, and that new information stands out to our conscious mind.

Even though we might not be aware of our 'dirt' hiding in plain sight, we'll certainly be aware of its *absence*.

~ Bradley

Four Horsemen: Shit-Pocalypse

What You Need To Know To Get Your Mind Back

I'll state the obvious: when we're at odds with someone or something, it's because of how we're feeling. We then look for ways to distract ourselves because the pain body interprets distraction as safety from our feelings.

But if you need to down a bottle of wine every night (like the *old* me used to), or use numbing prescription drugs every day (this was also me), or eat a whole block of chocolate in one sitting (the old me *loved* this), it's a sign that there's a wound in need of healing. It means our actions have us creating and building in a poor vibration. Our investment in negativity and distrust continues to grow, which only serves to intensify our feelings of stuckness and the behaviours we use to cope.

Luckily, we've got a better option.

We can learn to recognise where we collect our pesky shame from to resolve it. When we pause long enough to contemplate the root cause of our coping mechanisms, we see they're rarely random. They're signals meant to draw our attention to old wounds. Every destructive habit tells a story about where we've been hurt and how we're protecting ourselves from shame.

But applying our shame directly to our behaviours allows us to spot where and how it's been affecting our agreements or identity. Only then can we see what our 'four horsemen' create that isn't working for us.

Shame: The Catalyst

'No one wants to see that, darling.'

These were my grandmother's words whenever I wore clothing that exposed my legs. 'Don't show your husband anything because he'll leave you,' she'd say. 'He's too good for you.'

She taught me at a very early age that if I got fat, no one would love me. 'Your mother got fat, and look what happened. Your father left her. Don't do the same.'

She instilled in me a deep shame that I couldn't shake for most of my life. Do you think it contributed to my self-doubt?

You bet.

Did it affect my decision-making around particular events for most of my life?

You better *fucking* believe it.

We aren't born with shame built into our operating system. It results from being manipulated into behaving or holding beliefs that the unconscious self then views as true. Shame is an indicator that we've internalised someone else's perception of who we are or who we *should* be, and that we need to tune back into our *own* authenticity.

Someone might tell an upset child to 'suck it up, buttercup.' I heard this *often* growing up. Or perhaps, those nights at the dinner table when they were too full to swallow down the last few green beans on their plate, they had to endure statements like, 'people are starving in other countries… you're not leaving here until you're finished.' How about the age-old threat, 'I'll give you something to cry about,' when they weren't getting their way? Yep, that one can do some major damage. These remarks are *so* harmful because they destroy our sense of safety and replace it with self-worth-depleting feelings like shame.

Can you relate to any of these when you think back on your *own* childhood? How old were you? What did you feel during those moments?

Spiritually, shame is the misbelief that one is infinitely flawed, a mistake created by a higher power. Shame is our ultimate enemy. It's the internal sabre-toothed tiger we spend precious energy and sanity beating back. As I mentioned earlier, the most common limiting belief my clients come to me with is that they are not good enough, which often stems from pure shame. When we feel infinitely flawed or not enough, it's like saying to the source of all creation, 'You fucked it up.'

That's a destructive energy to foster.

In Ackerman and Puglisi's *The Emotional Wound Thesaurus* (2017), they call shame the lie that hides within a wound: 'The lie is a conclusion reached through flawed logic. Caught in a vulnerable state, the character tries to understand or rationalize his painful experience, only to falsely conclude that fault somehow lies within' (p. 6).

My son once had to catch my laptop in mid-air because I couldn't figure out how to use Zoom. Guess what? Shame: *why am I not smart enough to get this?*

A client's young daughter stopped drawing one day because her mother never provided the validation she'd been seeking for her art. *Mommy doesn't want to look at my picture because it's not good enough. I'm not good enough.*

At a cafe, my good friend knocked over his water glass and swore at himself, 'I'm such a fucking klutz.'

These examples of shame may seem trivial, but they matter. Every moment of self-shame carries weight. They can also compound, deepen and evolve into more intense limiting beliefs: *I'm not enough for you… I don't deserve the things I have… I can't be happy or healthy… I'm nothing.*

Shame isn't a beast we should feed. It creates trauma that our unconscious programming then responds to. And that is never helpful.

Rebranded, But Still Shame

Our bodies are full of pipes. The colon, intestines and arteries, all pipes! Even the brain has a minuscule pipe system for maintaining healthy function (Hays, 2022).

And like any pipes, ours can get clogged, kinked, knotted up or otherwise blocked. Each blockage has formed out of some deep-seated shame about who we are, and in order to heal, we must remove them. Until we do, the unconscious self will enact diversion methods to keep us operating despite these blocks.

Emotions and behaviours that look like shame:

- anger
- bitterness
- grief
- guilt
- sadness
- anxiety
- depression
- drama
- procrastination
- envy
- hatred
- resentment
- lying to oneself.

These are disguises of shame, and there is no deeper affliction than self-shame. It can be *horrible.* Believe it or not, they are easier to deal with than facing what's buried beneath; we actually prefer the above emotions and behaviours because our shame is about *us* and *not* somebody else.

Anger

Anger is perhaps the most common. People can still get shit done in a state of anger. It gets us out of bed in the morning, and the intensity distracts us from feeling shame.

Bitterness

Being bitter about someone else keeps us from looking at ourselves because it's easier to judge and blame others than face our shame.

Grief

When a loved one passes away, we grieve externally, but internally, we experience shame. That's a pretty ridiculous thing to consider, isn't it? Why would we feel shame in this instance? Because losing a loved one shatters our sense of security, and our programming causes us to self-blame for this entirely out-of-our-control event. Shame makes our grief about us: *I'm not good enough for you to stay alive for me.* It's the heart-wrenching feeling of abandonment.

Guilt

Guilt results from the relentless pressure of other people's expectations of us. When we fall short of their approval, shame seeps in. It's not just feeling bad about what we did or failed to do. We feel bad about who we are: *If I were better, I wouldn't have disappointed them.* At the core of guilt is shame, which convinces us we aren't enough.

Sadness

Why aren't I good enough for you to be different for me?

Not feeling good enough is a wound caused by unmet needs, such as a parent who didn't give us enough love or a friend who drifted away. Sadness mingles with the belief that if we *were* worthy, people would treat us better. It's shame convincing us that our pain is proof of our unworthiness or insufficiency.

Anxiety

Anxiety shows we're desperate to be in control of everything. When we experience panic attacks, it's a trauma response to feeling we have no control. And the root fear of losing control is shame.

Depression

When depressed, we feel so ashamed that we believe we can never win. It's a coping mechanism for hopelessness when we aren't living our soul-aligned purpose, not healing or not elevating.

Linked to feelings of failure and self-loathing, it shows us we're staying the same. It can become a deep, dark hole with no apparent way out.

Drama

What I consider the 'sleight of hand' of shame disguises, this is about pure distraction.

We use drama to draw attention away from ourselves and our shame: *look at that over there because what's over here is broken, and I don't want you to see it.*

Procrastination

Procrastination isn't laziness, contrary to popular belief.

It's safety. It's a coping mechanism for when *too* much is expected of us and we seek protection from feeling like we aren't good enough. Triggered by having to meet expectations set too high, we want nothing more than to avoid doing anything at all. We procrastinate rather than feel the shame of fucking up.

Envy

Worse than its sister emotion, jealousy, envy drives us to take something from another because we don't believe we can obtain it ourselves. Those with envy harbour massive amounts of shame.

Hatred

We use hatred toward others to deflect the hatred and shame we have for ourselves. When we feel unworthy or powerless, we often turn that discomfort outward, directing it at someone or something external to avoid facing our feelings.

Hatred is a false sense of control, and its intensity mirrors the depth of our self-judgement.

Resentment

Resentment shows us that we're living in the past and not allowing the present to be as it is. It requires massive amounts of energy to maintain. The behaviour consumes us from the inside, takes residence in the empty space, and then expands. It's one of the primary reasons we get sick. When resentment bleeds into our shame, it can affect us both mentally and physically (think stress).

It's a wall with living mortar. You can pull out a few bricks, but the holes will be filled in again.

Lying to Self

When we deny that anything is wrong, it's our programming trying to help us cope with the fact that things *are* wrong. We lie to ourselves, flat-out rejecting the fact that we feel shame.

The key here is to look past these disguises and unmask the shame lurking underneath. If we can't identify the blockages in our pipes and the core issues causing them, our automatic negative thoughts, feelings and beliefs will continue. Shame has a highly influential impact on our behaviour. When we disguise shame with the above, we miss the opportunity to heal old wounds that are causing our discomfort.

Self-Exploration: Shame Responses

An eye-opening yet straightforward way to identify when we fall into shame is to examine our current responses to specific situations. Take a few minutes to answer the following questions.

How do you react whenever you feel...

...sensitive?

...unappreciated or used?

...disrespected?

...like a perfectionist?

...like others are taking advantage of you?

...like you don't matter?

...like you're left out or can't be yourself?

Now let's imagine something better:

What would you do in these situations if you didn't react to the triggered shame?

Trauma: The Consequence

Picture this: I'm with a group of friends at the pool of a gorgeous, palatial resort. Everyone is in their swimwear and enjoying the crystalline water—everyone but me. In stark contrast, I'm layered from head to toe and sitting off to the side, watching, excluded from the fun by my own doing.

It isn't long before people notice my lack of participation. 'You alright, Emma? Come and join us!'

I flash them a masking smile. 'Oh, don't worry about me. I'm fine. Everything's fine.'

'What's wrong with Emma?' one of them says, tilting her head at a nearby friend. Unbeknownst to me, I've just triggered *her* shame. Mine has spread to her, and we're about to go into a shame cycle. 'Just get in the pool,' she shouts.

My participation will make her feel better, but it *won't* make me feel better. 'Stop fucking telling me what to do!'

BOOM! Now we're in a trauma cycle.

And it's all because my grandmother used to say to me, 'No one wants to see that, darling.'

Trauma comes from an event that damages our sense of safety and causes us to feel like victims trapped in a world of danger. It is a deep emotional response to an experience. As Iffland and Neuner (2026) suggest, trauma alters our coding and can establish recurring memories, fearful emotions, anxiety, panic, numbness, disconnection and other related behaviours.

Our primary trauma response types are:

- fight: confronting the threat
- flight: running away from the threat
- freeze: shutting down, or being unable to act
- fawn (people-please): calming or appeasing the threat.

It's important to note the difference between trauma and traumatic events, which usually involve an external threat to life or security. That said, any situation that leaves us feeling overwhelmed, isolated or unsafe can establish trauma, even things from the past or those imagined in the future.

That's worth repeating: *anything* that makes us feel unsafe can cause trauma.

Ambiguous Trauma

Sometimes, we're our own worst enemies. I know, brand-new information, right? When we go into a trauma response, it can only mean one of two things: either an actual danger is triggering us, or *we* are triggering ourselves based on a perceived threat that isn't actually real.

Triggers never happen for no reason. Never! If we go into a trauma response and there's no external threat nearby, it means we've unconsciously thought, said or acted on something that has affected us. We've put a crack through our *own* trust and safety. Have you ever been sitting in bed and suddenly felt nervous or uncomfortable? What were you thinking about? Chances are, it was something your unconscious self perceived as threatening, and it triggered a response. Nine times out of ten, this makes us think we've lost the plot.

We don't realise what *we're* doing to ourselves, that the negative thoughts and feelings are impacting our sense of security and our nervous system. Instead, we resort to unhealthy habits like prescription drugs or alcohol for relief.

Next time you feel anxious and can't pinpoint why, revisit what you were just thinking. Consider your words and what you might have been saying to yourself. If you were writing something down, what did it say?

Physical Effects of Unresolved Trauma

Everyone goes through some level of trauma, especially during childhood. Part of our healthy functioning is that our unconscious self builds survival mechanisms—notice that's not 'thrive' mechanisms—into our programs when we do. These behaviours help us make safe decisions so we can see tomorrow. Otherwise, you're *literally* crossing a six-lane freeway without watching the cars!

Shame is deeply connected to our experiences through the limbic system (Kaushal et al., 2024). It's the part of the brain that influences the autonomic nervous system regulation, which governs our trauma responses and triggers. Have a look at what can happen to the body when it enters a trauma response.

Can you relate to anything on this list?

- enhanced vision: pupils dilate, peripheral vision widens
- accelerated vitals: increased heart rate, breathing speed and blood pressure
- hormonal surge: release of adrenaline, noradrenaline and cortisol
- energy boost: blood flows directly to muscles, glucose floods the bloodstream
- heightened focus: increased alertness, reduced brain function (as low as twenty-five per cent)
- system shutdowns: reproductive and digestive systems deactivate
- heart risks: high blood pressure and heart disease
- hormonal overload: persistently high levels of cortisol and adrenaline
- physical strain: muscle tension, pain and fatigue
- gut issues: digestive problems like irritable bowel syndrome (IBS)
- mental exhaustion: burnout, insomnia, memory and focus issues
- emotional toll: anxiety, panic, depression and mood swings

- declining health: intensifying or even unexplainable reductions in overall well-being.

Trauma responses trigger the body into survival mode. Every energy source is diverted to help us fight back or escape. Also known as the 'defence reaction', the cardiovascular system becomes a heat map of stress hormones that affect the nervous system and our ability to relax (Fink, 2000).

We stop processing the food we eat.

We can't sleep.

Does this sound like a pleasant way to get through life?

Yeah, I don't think so either.

Legacy Pain

Imagine you're taking a walk on a sunny day. You're happy and feeling good. But out of the blue, you change course, zipping left to fast-walk down the next street.

Why did you just make that decision? More than likely, you felt a twinge you couldn't explain. A little 'uh-oh' rippled through you and innately redirected you out of harm's way.

That *innateness* is in your DNA. It's because some of your ancestors had to survive a traumatic event under similar circumstances, and that coding was built into your genetics to help keep you alive today. This invisible part of us is *fucking* powerful. Think back to your first year at school or being a teenager. How many times did you just innately know what to do? You didn't learn it; you were born with that unconscious knowledge. It's there for us even when we aren't consciously aware.

Trauma originates from various sources, including our DNA (Leif et al., 2019). We are born with embedded coding passed down from as far back as fifteen generations of our ancestral lineage (Abyzov et al., 2020; Jones et al., 2019; Leif et al., 2019). According to a study by Wharton et al. (2021), it's as high as one hundred and thirty-eight generations in other animals, which means we receive fragments of trauma that aren't even ours.

Considering what was happening in our ancestors' countries hundreds of years ago, it becomes obvious where trauma would have occurred and why those survival skills would be passed down generationally.

For me, I had to think back through nine generations of Irish Catholicism and follow a trail of seriously oppressive events, including slavery and signs that read, *No Blacks, No Dogs, No Irish.* We're all privy to innate knowledge because our ancestors endured significant trauma and managed to cope with it. If they hadn't, we wouldn't be here.

That said, it's important to remember that inherited trauma is not *our* trauma, and we don't *actually* need to know the exact moments or events that shaped it. Sure, we've got some of great-great-great-great-great Uncle Bertrand's DNA, but who knows what he was doing back in 1412! It's okay not to know because we can still elevate beyond it without those details. My clients prove that day in and day out during the incredible work we do together.

Agreements: Our Belief Shapers

Jason Parks and I have spent countless hours talking about agreements, and so much of my lived experience now reflects the impact of his teachings on this topic. See, I knew that shame leads to trauma and that people react based on their trauma responses, but I was unsure what happened after that. Then Jason shared this knowledge, and everything else just fell into place.

I'll be honest, it took a while for the concept to land. But once I understood that we could go into agreements with *energy*, the trauma cycle I was developing became complete.

Jason has a wonderful way of explaining energetic agreements:

Everything's energy—like floorboards. Every molecule of a floor is in a certain vibrational range, and that range is the agreement of those molecules. They're all holding that vibration, which is why we have the team. The sturdiness. If they were to change vibration, that would break down. So we wouldn't have that as a physical reality. We have that in everything, including the people we talk to, the relationships we have, all the shit we're carrying around. There is a level of agreement. And it can be a positive agreement, in which I can decide that I want to be a better version of myself. In doing that, I take action. I give my agreement mass. The more mass you add, the more weight it has—the more tangible it becomes. I can take all the necessary actions and align with the picture I have of myself. But if I sit in things like trauma, then I'm actually getting into agreement with the trauma. And I start adding mass to that instead. And it is actually that simple (Parks, 2024, p. 12-13).

That's massive! Even just considering something gives it density and the potential to form an agreement. The next time you catch yourself saying, 'Now, let's think about this… Let's Google that…' look at whether you're giving density to something positive or something negative.

Earlier, we touched on agreements and their package-deal nature. Consider this: if someone gives us a diagnosis and we say, 'Yeah, okay, I have dis-ease now,' we've just entered into an energetic agreement around the diagnosis. We also become energetically magnetic to anything on the same vibrational level.

For example, if I go into an agreement that I suffer from anxiety, I've just opened the door to attract everything in the realm of 'anxiety'. Think discomfort, hurt, poor business practises and not feeling good enough. What's worse, I won't even be aware it's happening. Unconsciously, I'm identifying as someone with anxiety and accepting that vibrational level, and soon, all of its shitty friends will join the party.

Agreement or Belief?

'If you've got time to sit down, you've got time to do something.'

I heard this from my mother throughout childhood, and it put me into a trauma response *every* time.

I developed a belief that I could people-please her by looking busy. Lo and behold, my unconscious self had agreed that I needed to be busy to please others. It wasn't true, of course, which I wouldn't learn for another forty-five years.

Nevertheless, I believed it.

People sometimes confuse agreements with beliefs, but they're very different. A belief is a conscious mindset, whereas an agreement is an unconscious bond to energy.

Let's say I love purple more than all other colours. You, however, like red more than purple. We end up arguing. 'Purple is a royal colour. It represents spirituality. Purple is everything!'

'Are you kidding me? Red is *so* much better than purple. It's *literally* the colour of our blood. It's the colour we're made of!'

Neither of us believes what the other is saying, so we'll keep going. Because my *belief* is what? Purple. And yours is red.

At that moment, what we don't realise is that we're in agreement with the *energy* of our argument. We want to prove ourselves right. Put each other down. Get angry. That's the agreement we have with the vibration of our conflict. I may disagree with what you're saying, but I'm most definitely in agreement with your energy.

Therein lies one of the dangers of energetic agreements, and a big part of what keeps us operating at low vibrational levels.

~

Much of my work with clients involves examining various aspects of their lives to uncover unconscious agreements and doubts. It's amazing when we find them because they then know what needs to be stopped and swapped. They can release what's keeping them in a negative frame of mind. The power of this work is in digging deep and being introspective. The more they embrace vulnerability and honesty, *without* self-shaming, the more they discover which energetic agreements can go.

Self-Exploration: Discovering Agreements

Take a few minutes to journal your thoughts on the following questions, being as honest and transparent as possible.

Which of my agreements are contributing to negativity in my life?

What new agreements would I like to adopt to enhance my sense of worth and self-love?

Identity: Unconscious Programs

It might not come as a surprise when I say we aren't aware of the vast majority of our decisions. That's why it's so important to examine our unconscious self.

Unlike our consciousness, which uses logic and facts for decision-making, the unconscious mind relies on past life events and learned survival techniques to make thousands of automatic decisions on our behalf *every single day*. It creates 'programs' from the thoughts, habits and beliefs we pick up at a very young age, sometimes before our first memory. Our brain then runs these coded programs on autopilot.

At any point, we're only aware of about five per cent of what's around us, including our own cognitive activity (Zaltman, 2003).

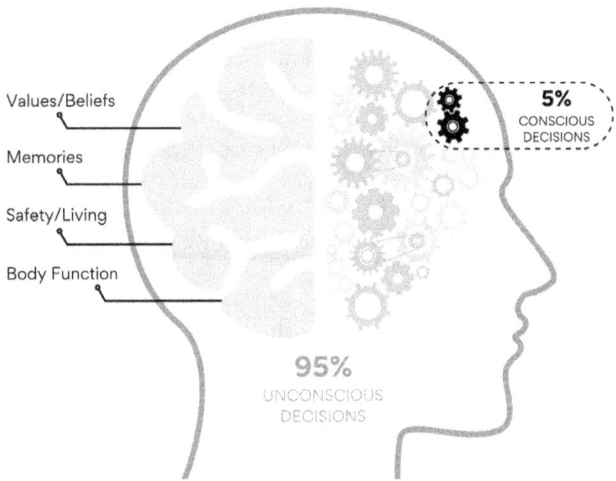

Graphic 6: Decision-making in the Mind

If you've settled into a comfortable chair while reading this book, you'll be aware of the seat beneath you. As you turn these pages, you'll *feel* the paper against your fingers. You'll *see* these black letters and know they form the words your mind is absorbing.

But what about the temperature of your pinky toe? Did you forget you even had one? Or a left knee? Are you aware of it now? And your back? I reckon you forgot all about it, and that's because it exists only in your unconscious mind until you remember it's there.

The brain is designed for efficiency. If we were conscious of every *single* thing around us and every decision we made, it would instantly overwhelm us. Therefore, the brain automates as many processes as possible to free up capacity for more complex tasks.

There are many things we don't need to be aware of once we know how to do them. Think about walking or riding a bicycle. Sure, you had to focus hard as you were learning. You had to be *fully, consciously aware* so that you could get it right. Once it became easy, however, you didn't have to think about it anymore. Your unconscious programming could just 'run' the 'walking program' or the 'bike-riding program' instead.

Most of our thoughts and decisions are the same. How we respond when someone teases us, how we feel about receiving instructions, or even what we believe is possible for our future, are all influenced by the programs running in the background.

Ninety-five per cent of our programs operate in the unconscious mind (Zaltman, 2003).

Think of the conscious mind like the boss of a large company: it can direct the unconscious mind. However, if the unconscious mind doesn't want to do it, it simply won't. This happens when change is involved, because our unconscious mind will always favour the familiar: familiar feels safe, and safety is a prime directive for our unconscious self. Consider the habit of smoking, although any habit or addiction can apply.

Consciously, a smoker will know it isn't good for them. It's expensive and leaves unflattering smells lingering behind. Numerous studies have proven it's a leading cause of cancer, like in the article, *Cigarette smoking and risk of second primary cancer* (Phua et al., 2022).

And yet, they'll go for that smoke anyway. Their unconscious mind will win a silent battle because the familiar is, 'We always smoke. It relaxes you. It's *you* time.' There's an identity hiding inside that feels safe because of their addiction.

Many people get trapped in the cycle of autopilot living. They may turn to things they don't actually desire but cannot seem to break free from, all because of their identity and programs. It's because their identity is the lens through which they perceive the world around them, or their 'forty bits of information' filter.

Automation Flaws

The unconscious mind can make our identity troubles worse for two reasons.

The first issue is that it can't distinguish between events happening *now* and those in the past. Our unconscious self does not understand time, and this can significantly impact which programs it chooses to run.

How many times have you mulled over a past event or speculated about a future one? When we think or talk about a horrible incident from the past, our body reacts as though that event *is* happening *now*.

The same applies when we think or talk about our future, even though it hasn't happened yet. The body floods with hormones that correspond to how we feel about our thoughts and the words we use. It's why a simple memory can hijack our whole day, even when there's nothing wrong in the present moment.

The second thing that causes us trouble is that our unconscious mind can't distinguish between talking about ourselves and talking about someone else. It simply responds to the tone of the conversation and thinks that we're shit-talking ourselves. Things such as gossip and criticism bounce negativity back into our own system whether we realise it or not.

If we think or say, 'I don't like that bitch,' our unconscious mind will respond as if we're talking about ourselves. Once again, the body releases hormones in response, even though we are *not actually* the topic of conversation.

In essence, the more we talk ill of others, the more our unconscious self feels victimised and throws our body into dis-ease. What might start as a thought, feeling or remark can quickly spiral into patterns that reinforce stress, tension and self-doubt.

The self-sabotage boomerang strikes again.

Unconscious Addiction to Misery

Has being right ever given you a little high? Ever felt good after an experience you know you absolutely shouldn't have? Do you love drama? Does it give a lovely boost of energy?

There's a scientific factor behind all of this, and it lies in a chemical called dopamine. Known as the feel-good hormone, it's responsible for creating neuroplasticity in the brain (Bono et al., 2020). Neuroplasticity enables us to change our brains and overcome past experiences.

Dopamine comes from the release of other hormones in the body, and this, my friend, is where we run into trouble. During one of my workshops with Dr Ashleigh Moreland, a neuroscientist and founder of the Re-MIND Institute, she explained the problem so well:

> *We can get dopamine from one of two pathways: oxytocin or cortisol, from either connection or threat. The really messed-up thing is that we can get dopamine from predicting correctly. So if, in our early life, we've experienced threat (cortisol) and things like hyper-vigilance, neglect, not being nurtured… and if there's a lack of connection (oxytocin), then we're predicting for the rest of our life that we get dopamine from dysfunctional, poor-attachment relationships, circumstances, employers and everything in our life. Suppose we experienced predictable nurturing, comfort, love, affection and attention in our early life. In that case, we will*

> *probably spend the rest of our lives seeking social connections, making friends, finding lovers and bonding at workplaces, as these interactions trigger a dopamine hit. That's off the back of oxytocin, whereas most people are wired to get it off the back of cortisol/stress. So they will create drama. They will set people up for failure because their brains are literally rewarded for doing it (Moreland, 2024, p. 7-11).*

This means that our unconscious programming can become coded to stress depending on our initial life experiences. It's why some people might continuously choose toxic relationships: they're *unconsciously* stuck in a loop of negative chemical wiring, even if it means they suffer.

Their programming reinforces their identity, which suggests they don't deserve anything other than what they've previously experienced. Consequently, they seek dopamine through stress and turmoil rather than happiness and calm. This chemical reward system of being 'right' provides the illusion of safety when, in fact, it's anything but. What a vicious, backward loop!

The 'Secondary Gain' Tactic

There's a not-so-funny motivator behind some of our unconscious behaviour, and it's fed by manipulation. It's what I call the secondary gain, or the connection *we* force out of others by expressing *our* shame in advantageous situations. It's a dangerous trap that can hurt those around us and nurture our addiction to misery.

Let's think back to the scenario of burning the toast and freaking out. Was there a secondary gain in this for me? Absolutely. My unconscious self knew exactly how to get sympathy from my family, and it was all in my self-deprecation: *I'm a fucking idiot. I'm so useless, I can't even cook fucking toast.*

I made sure my frustration had witnesses.

Guess who came racing to the rescue? My husband and my boys. I'd receive reassuring hugs and pats while they told me, 'You're not an idiot, Mummy. You're amazing. You're so smart.'

They'd reward me for bad behaviour, and I was in *full* agreement with it.

Once I became aware of this identity, I had to deconstruct and then replace it with healthier ways to acquire the connection I desired.

Secondary gains can manifest in almost any situation that's manipulable. Has someone ever introduced themselves and immediately followed with their new medical diagnosis? That's a subtle example of creating a connection through unconscious manipulation. And you'll know it worked if your response was something along the lines of, 'Oh no, that's *so* sad.'

I chose this example because I used to do this very thing.

Exploiting my illnesses to connect with people was another not-so-wonderful piece of my old identity. The secondary gain gave me energy and the *illusion* of safety in social settings because I already had an audience before I'd even stepped through the door.

When that gain came to light, I quickly fell out of agreement with it. Other people deserved my authenticity, and I deserved to know who I was without this identity of manipulation.

It was a line in the sand I was happy to draw.

~

So can we change these programs?

Can we alter our identity?

You betcha!

Getting in touch with our reactions and decisions helps us determine which aspects of ourselves to nurture and which to let go of. It takes practise and intention, but once we're able to step beyond our own limitations and conditioning, we can make choices from a place of clarity, authenticity and sovereignty.

Perfectionist Paralysis

Revisiting things we were told growing up can reveal identities we formed that do more than just operate in our unconscious mind. They might impose limiting beliefs, drag us straight into fear during specific events and keep us in lifelong avoidance cycles.

When I was a child, authoritative figures told me, 'If you're going to do something, you'd better do it right.' My teachers sometimes stated that perfection was the key to success. I watched as family members beat themselves up—and each other—over the tiniest flaw in their work and the simplest, most innocent mistakes.

I was younger than seven when these things started happening, and they formed an identity of perfectionism that I carried with me until thirty-seven. It shaped my belief that *perfection* was the goal, instead of authentic creation or actual productivity.

To me, it meant that anything but perfection equalled failure.

As a result, when confronted with tasks and activities that I couldn't do perfectly throughout my life, it caused damage. I abandoned half-completed colouring books if I strayed outside the lines. I stopped practising the piano when I struck a wrong note. I lost complete interest in school subjects when I received poor marks, like in the second grade, when my teacher gave me an 'H', which stood for 'Horrible'. And that's *exactly* how I felt about myself as I walked to the front of the class so I could observe it in the grade book.

I won't even get into how my fear of failure affected any budding athletic abilities. We'd be here forever.

Shame devastated me in every instance of imperfection. It kept me from trying new things as I got older and from participating in activities if I was unpractised. I had no motivation to try; if I couldn't do it perfectly, there was no point.

Or worse, what if I achieved something and others *still* perceived it as a failure?

Though I didn't know it, a coping mechanism for my feelings was developing in tandem with my shame: procrastination.

Suddenly, *not* taking action equalled safety. Avoidance *was* protection. Since success was hinged on perfection, I focused on my strengths and rejected everything else. I wound up diagnosed with anxiety to explain the procrastination, and then ADHD to explain the anxiety. It all spiralled and compounded from there.

The day I wrote this insert, I had to delve deep into core feelings and behaviours to examine what I was doing within myself. Every sentence of introspection I typed brought more clarity and more understanding. It was while writing this that I saw my identity for what it *truly* was.

In fact, before I'd even finished this paragraph, I'd decided to dissolve this identity of mine. Right then, things improved.

Did it mean the problem was rectified at that moment? No, but my *desire* for improvement was triggered. The *choice* to move forward was all mine.

And I chose change.

~ Bradley

Part Two

The Liberation Project: SSPA

Stepping Back Into Self-Leadership

'Believe in yourself. Trust the process. Change forever.'
~ Bob Harper

'The difference between misery and happiness depends
on what we do with our attention.'
~ Sharon Salzberg

'Sometimes we're not even aware that we're afraid. I know I wasn't...
'What would you do if you weren't afraid?''
~ Spencer Johnson, Who Moved My Cheese

'Unless we learn to know ourselves, we run the danger
of destroying ourselves.'
~ Ja A. Jahannes

'As he thinks, so he is; as he continues to think, so he remains.'
~ James Allen, As A Man Thinketh

Chapter Five

Stop It & Swap It

Reclaiming Authority, Revising The Narrative

It took me far too many years to realise we get to choose what to think, feel, say and do every second of the day. Whether at my worst or best, how I acted was my choice. I didn't know it at the time because my unconscious programming was busy making choices, but eventually, I woke up. When I did, I regained my sovereignty.

It's critical to remember that we're responsible for how we react to our thoughts and feelings. When that little voice creeps in and says, 'You can't possibly go to the gym today... You aren't good enough for this job... You're so useless...' we must disagree willingly. We can shut down the narrative quickly because we know it's not true.

If you're already finding an agreement, identity or action you could do differently, that's fantastic! It means your brain is lighting up in amazing and healthy ways.

When we ask ourselves what can change or what other possibilities exist, all the neurons in our brain go wild. They speak to each other and 'discuss' solutions to the new challenge. This 'discussion' affects our caudate nucleus, which acts as an identity filing system in the unconscious mind, and what we've stored there is not only important, but powerful (Doi, 2020).

Imagine your caudate nucleus has filed away an identity of *emptiness*. What could you possibly hope to create under this sort of identity?

How would your thoughts and feelings look?

Your inner dialogue?

It might sound like:

- 'I'm lonely and bored.'
- 'No one cares about me; I'll never get the love I need.'
- 'I can't find fulfilment.'
- 'It doesn't matter what I do today.'

And what about your results?

You might not do anything with your day. Perhaps you binge-eat or drink to feel both full and fulfilled. You might experience body pain. Then, as you look at the evidence in your results, you'll see it: emptiness is precisely what you've actioned. It's been your identity, and now it's your world.

Fuck that! It's time to stop and swap.

Graphic 7: SSPA Process

There's a wealth of scientific research that relates to this process, particularly the first two steps. A study from the University of Cambridge called *Improving Mental Health by Training the Suppression of Unwanted Thoughts* (Mamat & Anderson, 2023) found that training people to eliminate negative thoughts led to better mental health outcomes, including those with conditions like post-traumatic stress disorder

(PTSD). An article by Maureen Salamon, executive editor of *Harvard Women's Health Watch*, called *Break Free From 3 Self-sabotaging ANTs—Automatic Negative Thoughts* (2022) examined how cognitive reframing helps counteract automatic negative thoughts, influencing how we perceive situations in life. Recognising and reframing these thoughts is a crucial part of improving our mental well-being.

Complex medical jargon aside, SSPA is such an easy way to get yourself out of the shit and into a better state of living. I've been practising and sharing this process with my clients for ten years, with astonishingly powerful results.

Its application is so simple it seems almost foolish, yet it works.

It's because the unconscious mind likes simplicity, and our unconscious programs operate in an almost binary manner; they either run or they don't.

And it *all* has to do with speed.

Catch the Thought in 7 Seconds

How quickly can you stop the cycle?

We have mere seconds to make a conscious decision before our unconscious self chooses for us. When shitty thoughts invade our minds, they need to go as quickly as possible.

When we short-circuit our automatic negative thoughts, we:

- keep them from turning into feelings
- prevent hormones from releasing into our bloodstream
- keep unconscious programs from taking over
- prevent doubt and lies from becoming energetic agreements.

By wrenching ourselves away from our first or second negative thought *before* it becomes a feeling, we can freeze the particular program that triggers the release of hormones. Then, by thinking of something that gives us joy, we wind up triggering nicer feelings that lead to the release of better hormones.

By interrupting negative thoughts with something neutral, and even amusing, SSPA becomes quicker and easier, bypassing deep-rooted resistance.

I use a flamingo to ignite joy, and the reasons are:

- It's something entirely detached from myself and my reality.
- I have no personal relationship with it, or connection to it.
- I'm safe to picture it, suffering no unforeseen triggers.

If I had a pet flamingo at home, this wouldn't work.

If I were a zookeeper and looked after the flamingo exhibit, this wouldn't work.

If I lived in a part of the world where flamingos thrived, and I saw them every day, this *wouldn't* work.

Whatever your chosen anchor is, you *must* be detached from it. It should be natural, and you shouldn't have to think too hard to conjure it.

Don't use a pet or someone you know. Avoid anything that could cause you sadness or anxiety. Our mind is here to keep us safe, and it will surveil our surroundings for danger to ensure we aren't in harm's way. It's why we can't stop intrusive thoughts, but we *can* prevent our mind from setting unconscious programs into motion.

When Your Energy is Low, Lift It

Is it easy to raise our vibrational levels?

Sometimes, conjuring energy is the small spark that can ignite a whole current of change. And it can be as easy as envisioning something that outshines negative feelings. For me, it's flamingos. They represent a certain lightness. They hold a good vibration.

Do I know exactly what that vibration is?

Nope. And it doesn't matter. It could be joy, health or even undeniable *badassery*. Anything that lifts me instantly is the point. A tiny step in the right direction can be enough to create momentum and reveal new perspectives.

When we're stuck in negativity, we aren't the best problem-solvers. Marinating in misery is not an environment where solutions thrive. We first have to lift our vibration, and no, that doesn't mean repeating how much you love your job if you very much do not!

Let's go back to the flamingos.

They might seem like an unusual choice to some, but we don't have them in Australia and that makes them even more magical to me. You may also want to note that baby sloths are top-tier mood boosters.

But I digress.

The point is, the second I think of a sparkly pink flamingo, I've already moved up a few vibrational levels. And once I'm up, I can start shifting other things as well. Soon, I'm feeling less negative. I regain the ability to form and implement good ideas, such as taking a walk instead of going straight for wine.

That's progress.

Then, once I'm solid at this elevated level, I can do it again, climbing higher still.

Here's the thing, though: you've got to keep heading *up*. You must avoid thinking, feeling, speaking or acting in a manner that is contrary to your feelings. Think of it like a ladder: you don't want to move up three rungs just to come back down two. When every thought and word creates either a handhold or a slippery place to step, adopting visions and language that help you rise higher rather than sink back down is imperative.

If you've successfully lifted your vibration, don't sabotage it.

Don't put in the effort to improve your day and then tell your friend you had the worst morning, because you'll slip right back into those bad vibes.

Stay up.

Keep moving forward.

And if all else fails, think flamingos.

When Your Brain Stalls, Move On

What takes you from sad to glad?

When I need to stop a particular way of thinking, I'll order myself to do so out loud—no joke. Then, I'll immediately swap *in* something new, better, beautiful, ease-inducing and entirely distracting. Out with the bad, in with the good. Stop that werewolf in its tracks and swap it for a cute, harmless puppy.

Flamingos and all, this is my process.

We must stop the familiar that's imprisoned us. Our past should *not* dictate our future. The unconscious mind steers us into familiarity, so lay on that brake pedal and spin the car around. Pick an alternative route. Change that piece of your identity and say, '*This* is who I *really* am.'

Don't get me wrong, the goal of stopping and swapping isn't to erase our emotions. We're still allowed to feel what we need to feel because emotions are a major part of the human design.

However, we should ensure certain feelings don't persist or develop into an identity.

When Your Hormones Rush, Wait

How long does it take to come back down?

If you're unable to alter your thoughts and feelings before they cause a hormonal release, try not to panic! The effect of most hormones only lasts about ninety seconds, meaning you can still regulate out of a stress response with time.

A while back, my mother bought me a new toaster and simultaneously triggered the *fuck* out of me.

She walked into my home, the box in her arms, and said, 'Here, darling. I got you a new toaster.' A second later, she added, 'It's better than that other *shit* you buy.'

Her words were like a blow to the head, and I went into deep shame: *Why isn't my stuff good enough for her?*

My thoughts burrowed inward until Mum's gift felt more like a way of wounding me. Deeper still, and it stopped being about me entirely, becoming a conduit of Mum's *own* shame and her desire to be appreciated: *I'll make Emma feel extra-grateful that I'm so thoughtful.*

When the stress hormones kicked in, I was ready to fight. I wanted to bring down the whole damn house.

Luckily, my son pulled me out of the moment and dragged me into a side room. 'Don't say anything,' he told me. 'Just stop and swap.'

Begrudgingly, I did.

Instead of rage, I imagined flying around with a flock of sparkly flamingos.

It worked.

Even though I'd gone past the hormone release phase, it brought me back down. Ninety seconds later, my body regulated, and my nervous system relaxed.

The fog of anger left my head. And just like that, it was over.

From Victimhood to Responsibility

When we slip into blame, who holds our power?

The more common concept of responsibility encompasses aspects such as duty, obligation and leadership (Cioffi, 2015).

However, there's another side to it that applies *internally*, and it involves qualities like maturity, rationality, level-headedness and trustworthiness. Internally, responsibility is simply our ability to choose how we respond to things.

Simple right?

It's the autonomy of our consciousness, meaning we must own our reactions, both good and bad.

For instance, how might you respond to an anxious thought? Would you fall into agreement with it? Let it turn into anxiety and become a part of your identity?

Or would you knock it back and stay sovereign?

Our responsibility lies in the choices we make and how we move forward afterwards. When our response keeps us trapped in negative states, it means we've fallen into a state of *victimhood*. It means our trauma is getting the better of us.

Just as there's a distinction between trauma and traumatic events, so too does victimhood differ from being a victim. When someone or something victimises us, it's external victimisation.

However, victimhood is internal.

It's a state we put *ourselves* into.

It's a tricky agreement because it's how we're taught to view situations of misfortune.

Victimhood leads us to shift away from active responsibility and towards blame instead. The moment our language turns outward, or we catch ourselves saying things like, 'He made me feel this way… It's her fault…' we know we've chosen to operate from a place of disempowerment and denial.

I had a *horrendous* relationship with my father.

Even after some distance, I still played the part of his victim for a long time, re-traumatising myself each time I revisited the past. I felt and acted as if certain transgressions that had occurred during childhood were *still* happening.

What's scary to contend with is that if I'd kept blaming my father, I wouldn't have changed. Instead, my whole life would have been spent in victim mode, waiting for him to change. The trauma would have lingered, raw and damaging. My unconscious self and my soul wouldn't have healed, and I'd never have risen back into responsibility.

While I'm not responsible for my father, I *am* responsible for how I choose to live my life. Believe me when I say I understand what a tough call this can be. When responding to shitty events means having to hunt for things like forgiveness and hidden wisdom, our unconscious self says, 'No way. You're the victim here, remember?'

But trauma breaks us apart, so we have the chance to step out of victimhood and create ourselves anew. Otherwise, we remain in victimhood, repeatedly experiencing the same trauma in different forms.

I stopped identifying with the word *victim* long ago because victimhood does nothing but disempower us and strengthen our limiting beliefs. We stop thinking that life *can* change and wait for the world to change instead.

So let's banish that agreement here and now because it simply isn't true. Although we can't alter past trauma, we can still act with healthy responsibility to build a better future for ourselves.

Results

What story are they telling?

If we want to know how our life is going, it's in our results.

Pretty simple, right?

Jason Parks and I often spoke about this on our co-hosted podcast, *Soul Aligned Results*. Because results. Are. *Everywhere*. They're in your bank account. The clutter in your home. The state of your purse or backpack. They could be affecting your physical and mental health, as well as the kinds of relationships you've been magnetising. They're contributing to how you feel.

What our results reveal can be pretty sobering. Once again, the trick to reading them is introspection. Getting real with yourself is how you discover what needs to be stopped and swapped. We must follow the evidence of our behaviours and actions so that we know what we've achieved, or where there's a need for improvement.

Have you opened your closet recently? Did you find it stuffed full of things you didn't remember having? You might be a 'shover', like I was. I shoved all sorts of shit into my closet until I couldn't fit any more in. It was the result of suppressing my *own* greatness and doubting my right to success.

I don't do that anymore.

In fact, my old agreement of 'undeserving' is long gone.

The same can apply to our interactions with others. For example, when I get angry at my son for his tone, it means there's actually something *I* need to look at, something that I'm being shown. It isn't about him, but a *mirror* moment.

When confronted by a trigger, my agreement is that I look deeply into my own shame first. I know there's a lesson to be learned. I self-reflect on where I might be treating myself the same way or where I'm not being kind to myself.

And I'll find something. I always do.

That uncomfortable external experience helps me recognise when and how I drift off course. There wouldn't be a need for my son's disrespect if I didn't need a lesson. Don't get me wrong, I'd still address his tone, but I'd do it in a way that doesn't spark a shame cycle or make shame the reason he apologises.

Just like that, I've received results in real time. The evidence is in the apology and the shift in tone for the rest of the day.

Just as our results show us what *isn't* going well, they can also prove what *is*. One of the best ways for us to do this is by telling ourselves how we're succeeding. Glean motivation from the evidence because *knowing* we're getting some things right is empowering.

Imagine the last time you told somebody you were proud of them or showed them proof of their success. How did they change in the moment?

Did they stand a bit taller?

Were they all smiles?

Did they hug you?

Giving ourselves positivity has the same effect. You deserve to recognise, celebrate and share your *own* results. When you do, your vibration changes. More so, you affect the vibrational frequencies around you.

What Are You Absorbing?

If we aren't leading, then who or what are we following?

Would you believe a person can be triggered by what they view on social media every single second?

Not only is it true, but the effects can be catastrophic.

Continuous triggers lead to negative feelings compounding throughout the day, keeping us locked in a trauma response. In fact, scrolling a smart device first thing in the morning has a higher chance of sabotaging the course of our day than a bad night's sleep.

Yikes!

According to Katella's Yale Medicine article, *Social Media and Teen Mental Health: A Parent's Guide* (2024), the fast-paced nature of social media, with its mix of positive and negative content, can cause teens to experience mood swings, stress and continuous emotional triggers. Considering the technology's design, particularly the algorithms that prioritise sensational, reactionary and emotionally charged content, the effects are understandable.

And what's worse, we can become addicted to these effects because of the hormones they trigger in us.

What influences us has massive power and affects lifelong programs. It's important to consider what may be affecting you and in what ways.

Our major influencers include:

- family: we pay close attention to their behaviour, speech and perspectives

- school and society: we're taught social norms and ideologies that frame our cultural identities and values (these ideologies are typically shaped by the experiences, trauma, biases and paradigms of previous generations)
- media: informs our perception of culture, social interaction and opportunities, good or bad
- inherent survival mechanisms: we react to events that code our unconscious programs, shaping our emotional responses to recreate pleasurable experiences or avoid painful ones (these programs can even be pre-coded through our ancestry)
- religion: we're conditioned to practise, even obey without question, religious doctrine to prevent disapproval and gain social acceptance and safety
- emotions: we learn how to make decisions based on a desire, even when the original circumstances are no longer relevant.

Letting Go of Control

The TV channel analogy

Imagine you've got a remote control for your whole life, and the various directions you can take your life are the TV channels you get to choose from. Each channel brings its own style, content, vibe and influencers.

Let's choose one.

What kind of content is shown on the news channel?

Death, destruction and war? Not ideal for a high-vibration life, so let's leave that one alone.

If we flip to the 'fun' channel instead, what do we get? Good vibes, of course! In fact, there are a hundred different programs on that channel every week, so this is good. It fits our vision of a positive and abundant life.

Unfortunately, we tend to get picky with the programs on the 'fun' channel, frustrated because we can't just choose our favourite programs and scrap the rest. We stop holding the vision of 'fun' and insist on trying to do the network producer's job instead. But what's *showing* on the channel is not up to us. How our 'fun' is fulfilled is not ours to control. That's the job of our higher self, of Source, and we have to trust in that. When we try to control everything on the 'fun' channel, we often impede our manifestation efforts.

The reality is we may not *actually* know what our ideal fun is meant to be, and that's okay. The vision keeps us tuned into the vibe, and the network producer, Source, ensures we have another program lined up after this one finishes. All we need to do is sit there and embody 'fun'.

A key to achieving success in relationships, financial stability, business ventures, health or any other area is visualising and holding onto it. That, and not getting in the way of what it might look like.

It will come to you if you let it.

When we try to play the role of network producer, it overwhelms us.

Leave it to the powers that be. To Source.

Just hold the vision and trust the rest will come.

Self-Exploration: Identifying Your Results

Take a few minutes to reflect on your results.

Answer the following questions and see if any patterns or similarities become noticeable.

If my bank account were a person, I'd describe 'them' as…

If my closet is a reflection of my mind, it currently looks…

When I look in the mirror, I think and notice…

The friends I hang out with are always so…

Looking around the room, I can spot (   ) things that are out of place…

Right now, I feel about myself…

Ease Over Hardship

Contrary to popular belief, we weren't made for a life of struggle. We don't exist to endure shitty relationships, poverty or poor health. We weren't born just to put the financial success of a corporation, or everyone else's needs, for that matter, before our own. We're meant for a life of ease.

But ease is the exact *opposite* of how we've been taught to think about life. It's why envisioning a better way forward can be *so* tricky. We're quick to accept those low-vibration thoughts, feelings and identities because our parents, bosses, teachers and religious leaders have *literally* conditioned us to do so.

So, we self-sabotage; it's a cultural norm, after all.

We surrender to shame, old trauma and our past. We accept and maintain agreements of suffering. Martyrdom. We often find ourselves in lifelong fights that we can never win.

I used to slither out of bed late, skip the shower, swear, flash a few eye-rolls at the mirror, down four shots of coffee and brace for another shitty day. These were the conditions of my identity, my agreement that the next eighteen hours would be just another slog, remedied later by a bottle of tequila before lights out.

In other words, I *fucked* it up. I failed myself daily.

Nothing stopped, nothing swapped.

The result? Misery.

It was during a wave of deep dissatisfaction that I wondered why my life had become an endless uphill battle. The answer came quickly. Unconsciously, it was how I believed life should be.

These days, my agreements look very different. My life is now a flexible balance of hard work and ease. I make room for kindness and self-love because they soften hardship and promote my well-being. I *want* to get out of bed in the morning. I get to be productive, and I look forward to the journey and subsequent results that prove I've grown.

The best part of this shift? Nothing changed except my perception of the problem and sense of responsibility.

So if in the morning, the first thing you see in the mirror has you saying, 'Oh God, that's gross,' ask yourself why self-love is so hard? If you're embarrassed by your life instead of proud, dream of what your life could look like. Don't reinforce your limiting beliefs by indulging in negativity. Don't use your power to nourish shame.

If you have blocks in your metaphorical pipes and kinks in your hoses, then get determined because you can 'unkink' them. And how amazing is that? You just have to know what the kink is.

As Emma frequently says, 'It gets difficult when it's untrue and easier when it's true.'

Hardship will make us feel like the joker, maid or stable boy of our own castle. But ease will make us the king or queen.

- Bradley

Chapter Six

Get Present

Stepping Out Of Your Time Machine

There's a widely regarded concept around conscious presence: when we aren't living in the moment (Andrews-Hanna, 2011), it means we're either stuck in the past or chasing the future.

Neither is helpful, especially when we're stopping and swapping. The past *isn't* happening to us anymore, and the future *hasn't* happened at all. So, why do we insist on visiting either?

Certain mindfulness practises can keep us grounded in the present moment (Coyne, 2024), which is crucial for mitigating the impact of our negative thoughts and preventing us from spiralling into past regrets or future anxieties. It's why getting present is included in SSPA.

The importance of staying present is like being at home so that you can receive deliveries. We may as well be on holiday when our minds float around in the future. Our 'house' is left empty, with no one to answer the door.

When we get stuck in the past, we're in the dark. Our porch light is off, and the delivery truck keeps driving. The universe is *always* supportive and giving, but we must be 'home' to receive its gifts.

If I ask the universe for things like money, health and a good career, I'd better be around when Source brings them to my front door!

When we go visiting the past or future, we usually wind up in shitty memories or made-up scenarios that trigger our unconscious self. We then think, feel and react to things like fear, regret, trepidation, anxiousness, vulnerability and any other triggers.

Meanwhile, the gifts we've been asking for pass us by, unnoticed.

We can't be at home within ourselves when we aren't living in the present. When we're too busy focusing our attention elsewhere to see the delivery van parked in our driveway or hear the doorbell ringing, we lose out. It means the universe is just standing on the porch steps with a stack of parcels, shrugging its shoulders.

Well, guess what? Someone else *is* home, and they'll be all too happy to collect instead.

When Your Mind Drifts, Look Around

What brings you back to the present?

It's safe to say that staying present one hundred per cent of the time is about as likely as a teenager keeping their bedroom clean.

When we aren't paying attention, our minds wander, time-warping into the past or future. However, here's a simple trick for getting back into the *now*. It seriously doesn't get easier than this.

When you catch yourself drifting, take five quick seconds to look around. As you do, just start naming the things you see nearby: 'Mug, phone, TV, chair, napping cat...' It shouldn't be poetic or profound, just obvious.

Congratulations! You've just returned from your mental time travel. Well done!

'How does that possibly work?' you might be asking. Well, when you're preoccupied with spotting and naming objects, you're too busy to overanalyse past regrets or future problems. Your brain can only focus on one thing at a time, and right now it's that half-empty coffee cup on the end table. You're very aware you're in your home, which is great. When you're home, you're present.

The past and future are just stories your mind tells you. The present is the only place where life is *truly* happening, and all it takes to get back there is a simple inventory of your surroundings—no time machine required.

SSPA Exercise: Coming Home to Self

Take five seconds to bring yourself back to the present:

- Be a 'bird' and hunt for objects around you.
- Say what you see out loud (television, dog, etc.).
- Feel your mind leave the past and the future and return to the present moment.

It's Not Happening Now

Are we revisiting the past or looking from the future?

Most of our issues stem from two sources: past experiences or fears about the future. Despite how it can feel, these things aren't *actually* happening right now. But the longer we linger in the past, the more it shapes our future to look exactly the same.

Do you have people in your life who always whine about the same old thing? Mine is my mum complaining about her knees. She keeps telling herself she has bad knees. Then, she wakes up the next morning and confirms it.

Naturally, I tell her, 'You keep thinking about how bad they were yesterday, so you're just inserting that expectation into today and tomorrow.'

She agrees, of course. Because she's one hundred per cent right.

'If you had the healthiest knees in the world,' I ask, 'what's the worst that could happen?'

She doesn't even hesitate: 'I'd have to exercise.'

And there it is, the *real* problem.

Another example is when my son was ten, and a classmate bullied him.

For the next decade, that experience worked in the background to shape his entire world. His communicator body latched onto it, using it as an excuse for everything. The result is that while no one is bullying him today, he lives as if someone still is. And that's shame, the deep, heavy kind that whispers, *Why am I not good enough?* For my son, it was, *Why wasn't I good enough for you to stop bullying me?*

The emotional toll of bullying was *massive.* The trauma response was *tremendous.* He shut down and pulled away. He couldn't go to school for weeks. We moved him to a new school, which helped, but by then his communicator body had already coded a new unconscious program that said, 'Now we know what to do! Any time we wind up in discomfort, we'll just freeze until something changes.'

Newsflash: that solution works for about five minutes.

Let's fast-forward to today. Any time my son thinks about trying something new, his communicator body jumps right in: 'Oh man, you're joking, right? Don't forget, you're still being bullied!'

But he's not.

He hasn't even seen the boy since he was ten. And that's the real 'a-ha' moment. It's not about what happened, but what he does with it now. When we let an event *own* us, the person involved also owns us. My son wasn't just bullied; his aggressor owned his life, future and choices.

Pretty ominous, considering the boy wasn't even in the picture.

~

So, who or what owns you? If you struggle with anxiety, depression or anything in that realm, what's *really* going on? You might be stuck in the past, responding as if an old event is still happening.

Ask yourself: 'What went down when I was a kid that I'm still carrying around like an open wound?' Because *that's* shame, and when you sit in shame, guess what? The information your conscious mind takes in every second gets filtered through it.

It means no one can rescue you. You're tuned into the wrong frequency to see things like love, care and support.

I have to ask myself this question constantly, and then urge myself to let it go: *Emma, stop acting like what happened between zero and seven is still happening. Stop revisiting the horrible treatment you received from your father. Stop behaving as if your first husband still beats you.*

To this day, I catch myself acting like I'm in school with that one dickhead teacher who *always* told me I wouldn't amount to anything. Well, you know what? I don't even know him anymore. Sometimes we just need to give ourselves a good kick in the arse and say, 'That's not happening anymore, babe.'

Our communicator body *loves* selling us the sob story of *look what they did to me,* when what we really need is to embrace the truth: *holy shit, regardless of them, I'm still bloody awesome.*

A practitioner in training once asked me why we hold on to the shit. The answer is simple: for proof.

Proof that we can survive anything.

Proof that we're resilient and resourceful.

Proof that, no matter what, we can keep going.

And it's when we've accumulated enough of that proof that we realise we're unstoppable.

That doesn't mean life won't hit you with curveballs; rather, when the next one comes, you won't crumble from the impact. You'll stand up, dust off and say, 'I know how to handle this. I've been through worse, and I'm still standing.'

And that's powerful. That's freedom.

The past is just *stuff.* We already have everything we need at this moment, but we hold on to old stories as if they were gospel. We must stop dwelling on the pain of things that have come and gone.

From the Case Files: The Shadow Man

A client came to me because he was destroying his marriage. He lived in a cycle of deep childhood shame because of his mother, who he stated never loved him.

Every time he experienced this shame, it triggered his trauma response: he froze, shut down and shut out his wife. It caused him to avoid leading and making decisions—a responsibility typically passed back and forth between spouses to maintain balance. He became a mere *shadow* in his own life.

What he didn't realise was that he had an unconscious agreement to this type of disowned energy.

I asked him to imagine being married to someone who was constantly in a trauma response and stuck in the past.

He said it would be exhausting.

I explained this was the reality for his wife when his coding overrode his ability to be an equal partner in the relationship; that his marriage was unstable because she kept having to fulfill the role of both husband and wife; that while he behaved like he still wasn't receiving love, he was negating the love she had for him; that he had to find a way to release his feelings of shame and get back to the present moment.

It took a few sessions, but he did it.

And once he came back from the past, his relationship rapidly changed.

His nervous system had regulated.

He and his wife fell back in love, and they finally went on their honeymoon.

Today, he's better than ever.

Breathwork

How does less gasping & more grounding sound?

Breath is the *most* powerful tool we have for regulating the nervous system. It makes the SSPA process more effective by connecting the mind and body, drawing us back to calm, clarity and the present. When we're aware of our breath, it's like saying to our unconscious self, *You're safe. There's no need to worry.*

This breathwork alone can be enough to shift us out of a trauma response, so imagine the impact it can have through SSPA! The beauty of breath is in its simplicity. We don't need hours of practise or special equipment to harness its power. All we have to do is ensure we breathe deeply and fully into the belly. Forget shallow breathing altogether.

This deeper type of breathing, called diaphragmatic breathing, is how we're *supposed* to breathe.

And it comes with some major benefits:

- activation of our 'rest and digest' system
- better oxygen flow
- reduced tension and overwhelm
- emotional regulation
- promotion of our physical health (Xiao et al., 2017).

Here's how breathwork has helped some of my clients:

1. Client A struggles with anxious thoughts. She uses SSPA and her breath as an anchor to regain control. She stops, takes three slow breaths and pictures something amusing, which reduces her anxiety and *short-circuits* her stress response. Over time, this simple practise has helped her nervous system become less reactive, making her feel calmer and more in control.

2. Client B utilises breathwork and the SSPA process to remain composed during important meetings. Instead of freezing up, he stops, swaps and practises conscious breathing, calling it his 'secret superpower'.

3. Client C utilises breathwork to manage overwhelming feelings of guilt and self-criticism. She stops, swaps the guilt with a lighthearted visual, and breathes deeply. This simple shift helps

her move beyond the past, elevates her vibrational level and reinforces self-compassion.

4. Client D deals with many tense family gatherings, relying on breath and SSPA to get through them. When frustration rises, he takes slow, grounding breaths and imagines something ridiculous. These grounding breaths help him respond calmly instead of losing it. As a result, he approaches conversations with more patience, reducing conflict and fostering stronger relationships.

Here are four additional breathing techniques:

1. 'Box' breathing: inhale for a count of four. Hold for four. Exhale for four. Hold for four. Repeat the cycle four times. This method is simple and effective for calming the nervous system or regaining focus and composure.

2. '4-7-8' breathing: inhale for a count of four. Hold for seven. Exhale slowly through your mouth for a count of eight. Repeat at least three times. This method eases anxiety while promoting deep relaxation and better sleep.

3. Alternate nostril breathing: first, use your thumb to close your right nostril and inhale through your left. Then close the left nostril with your ring finger and exhale through the right. Then, inhale through the right nostril, close it and exhale through the left. Repeat for several cycles. This ancient practice soothes the nervous system, promotes balance and aids mental clarity.

4. Resonant breathing: inhale for five seconds. Exhale for five seconds. Repeat for at least one minute. This method of rhythmic breathing is ideal for stress management, aligning the heart rate and calming the nervous system.

Breathing is always available to us, and it's when we make it intentional that we're able to utilise its power in great ways. Every inhale and exhale is an opportunity to calm our mind and body. Then combined with SSPA, it acts as our way back to the present.

Breath is the navigator we often take for granted, so trust in its power because it won't steer you wrong.

10 More Ways to Get Present Fast

The 5-Word Check-In

Pause and describe your current state in just five words. This forces quick self-awareness without overthinking.

Example: 'Calm. Focused. Slightly hungry. Alert.'

The Next Tiny Step

Ground yourself by focusing on the smallest next action you can easily take.

Small actions will keep you engaged with what's right in front of you.

Example: 'Open the document... Take one sip of water... Format the heading...'

Sensory Subtraction

Block out one of your senses temporarily. Now notice how it heightens your awareness of the others.

What details emerge?

Examples: closing your eyes, wearing earplugs, holding your breath.

Internal Weather Report

Ask yourself, 'What's the weather like inside me?'

Identifying your internal state, much like a forecast, makes it *easier* to acknowledge and then shift.

Examples: cloudy, stormy, warm, icy.

The Stream-of-Consciousness Snapshot

Pause and record the uncensored thoughts in your head for one minute. Witness your mind in raw motion as it acts in the present.

Examples: flow writing, voice recording, sketching or doodling.

Streetlight Musing

Find a small, mundane object nearby and study it as though it holds some great hidden meaning, like a clue in a puzzle.

Examples: a crack in the sidewalk, a lamppost, a piece of litter.

Microadventures

Step outside and walk a random path without a destination. See where it takes you.

Let curiosity guide your movement.

Examples: follow a colour, sound, animal or intriguing object.

Reality Refit

Change one small thing about your environment or routine to shake your perception. Notice how it shifts your awareness.

Examples: wearing mismatched socks, eating breakfast for dinner, taking a shower in the dark.

Talk to an Object

Pick a random object nearby. Suspend disbelief and strike up an imaginary conversation. What would it say? What has it seen?

Examples: chatting with your coffee mug, consoling a houseplant, interrogating the dish sponge.

Become a Ghost for Five Minutes

Mentally erase your identity. Forget your name, job and history.

Just exist as a nameless presence, experiencing the raw now with no story attached.

Example: wander through a familiar space like a stranger.

Bonus: Live Your Own Movie

Be your own main character and experience life like a film scene unfolding before you.

Example: narrate your day like a movie script.

Self-Exploration: Here & Now

Take a few minutes to journal or sketch about these questions that are meant to ground you. Ponder the present and let yourself fully arrive at this moment.

What do I notice about my life when I come back from the past or future?

What do I think and feel when I'm truly home within myself?

What gifts and/or opportunities are waiting for me in the present?

Daily Presence Through Daily Ritual

Personal rituals not only promote routine but also reduce stress in our nervous system and help alleviate overwhelming feelings. They allow the brain to take a break from worry and stop us from wandering into the past or future.

The best ways to achieve presence are all about simplicity. Whether we're taking a cool shower, savouring a cup of coffee or going for a dip in the ocean at sunrise, it's the *intentional* action that grounds us and reconnects us to the real world.

Here are some of my favourite screen-free rituals:

- Preparing a cup of matcha in the morning: the slow, methodical process sets a mindful and productive tone for the day.
- Beautifying a plant: watering or pruning a plant connects me to nature and fosters a caring mindset.
- Cleaning my reading glasses: this minor act sharpens my focus, both literally and figuratively.
- Mindful movement with my dog: on a short walk, I can be fully aware of the sights, sounds and sensations around me.
- Lighting sage or sustainably sourced palo santo: this sensory and energy-cleansing ritual promotes a conscious shift in energy and attention.
- Breathing exercises: structuring my breathing allows stillness (follow the guided breathing techniques in 'Breathwork').
- Creating something: anything! Even a few words in a journal can be an act of presence and expression.
- Sunrise or sunset reflection: taking a moment at the start or end of the day to recall an experience I *truly* felt immersed in brings a sense of accomplishment and peace.

By incorporating small, mindful rituals like these into our day, we establish routines that bring us more presence, fulfilment and inner peace.

We don't have to get rigid with our routines, as inflexibility can lead to feeling pressured. We want the opposite: to create gentle pauses that bring us back to ourselves, one intentional breath, step or sip at a time.

- Bradley

Chapter Seven

Take Action

It's Not Magic, It's Mass & Momentum

The final step of SSPA is the one that cements the process's cumulative effects in place. Deliberate action is the quickest way to wipe out well-ingrained habits. It reinforces new behaviours and beliefs. The caudate nucleus fires up to facilitate learning and help integrate new information (Chiswo, 2024).

Earlier in this book, we touched on how our neurons become excited when we think about possibilities. They begin to look for different ways of doing things. Breaking our pattern of thought is crucial to this new activity in the brain; otherwise, our neurons continue to align with what's familiar. They're primed to follow patterns, good or bad.

Let's be real: even with SSPA, we'll end up with the occasional negative thought and feeling. After all, we're human beings with emotions and communicator bodies. The real skill here is not acting on those thoughts or feelings. Just as we get to choose our responses to things, we also get to choose the kind of action we take. Therefore, our conscious actions need to steer us in the opposite direction to what our unconscious self thinks is safe.

From the Case Files: Unexpected Action

A wonderful mum recently came to me with her young daughter, who'd entered a rebellious phase after her father left due to his alcoholism. She described the ordeal as sad, frustrating, incredibly overwhelming for them and a situation that has left her daughter lashing out on social media and stirring up negativity.

I explained that her daughter was using social media as a distraction to avoid dealing with her feelings. I suggested she use SSPA instead. Together with her daughter, we devised a plan that would be even easier than using an app to vent her frustrations.

First, she'd stop herself. Then, she'd look around and say to herself, 'I'm safe and loved.' As she did this, she'd imagine a basketball with a toupee and moustache. When we got to the 'action' step, the daughter planned to do pushups.

Instead, I urged her to think of something else. Something she never does.

She agreed on humming a tune instead.

Now, she doesn't need social media as a coping mechanism. She's adopted SSPA in its place.

The Magic of Unusual

How do we achieve effective action?

Want to shut down a negative pattern fast?

Get weird.

Effective action means doing something unusual enough to disrupt your flow of thought, and positive enough to keep you from downgrading your vibrational level (you don't want to yell at someone or kick over chairs). It *literally* needs to interfere with your regular pattern.

For my young, rebellious client, that meant humming to herself. The break in routine then allowed for new thoughts to germinate.

Despite its simplicity, humming can be a *powerful* tool for short-circuiting negative thought patterns and shifting emotions.

It works by:

- activating the vagus nerve, which helps you transition from a stressed state to a calm one
- releasing tension with physical vibrations that soothe your body
- improving mood by increasing the flow of oxygen and triggering feel-good hormones like serotonin
- disrupting the pattern of behaviour allows you to abandon an automatic emotional response and create a new one (Kolk, 2014).

Choosing to hum a tune worked for my client because it was something she never did. The unfamiliar action severed the connection between her feelings and the act of seeking negative attention.

This change in focus helped her choose a different, more positive response that avoided frustration and social media.

10 Ways to Break Negative Patterns Fast

Speak in a Funny Accent

Say, 'I am safe and loved,' in the silliest accent you can.

It's pretty hard to stay stuck in a negative loop when you're laughing at yourself!

Examples: Elvis, a pirate, a robot, a cartoon character.

Dance Like a Maniac

Get silly because it'll jolt you right out of an emotional funk.

Example: throw on a random song and dance wildly for thirty seconds.

Sound Bursts

Clap your hands and shout something silly. The physical action coupled with an unexpected word will be confusing enough to disrupt an emotion or feeling.

Examples: 'chinchilla', 'bubblegum', 'SpongeBob'.

Power Pose

Hold a pose for thirty seconds. This will boost confidence and shift your energy.

Example: throw your arms up like you just won a marathon.

Blow Raspberries

It's goofy, unexpected, and can physically release tension around the jaw and throat, where we often hold stress.

Example: stick your tongue out and blow raspberries like a baby. I'm not joking!

Spin in a Circle

It'll disrupt mental focus, shifting attention to your body rather than your negative thoughts.

Example: spin in place three to five times.

The Compliment Game

This can instantly interrupt repetitive thought loops.

Example: find an item nearby and give it three sincere or silly compliments.

Sing Instructions to Yourself

Sing your next action like you're in a musical. Even if it's simple, it will shift your brain into a lighter, more creative state.

Examples: getting a glass of water, loading the dishwasher, picking an outfit.

High-Five Yourself in the Mirror

This small action builds a connection to self and lightens the emotional load.

Example: walk up to a mirror, give yourself a gentle high-five (don't break it!) and say, 'I've got this.'

Hop on One Foot & Name Foods

This movement, combined with the cognitive challenge, works because it engages both the body and the brain, much like the 'Sound Bursts' method.

Examples: watermelon, beef jerky, sourdough, Worcestershire sauce.

Undoing Negative Anchors

What keeps us 'run aground'?

As we go through life, we unknowingly develop energetic habits and 'hotspots' in our environment. They're born out of repeated behaviours and their matching vibrational levels. These energetic and often psychological triggers are known as anchors. Anchors link things in our environment, such as a place, sound, smell or even someone's voice or tone, to our specific emotional states and responses (Bell et al., 2025). And like anything, these triggers can be positive or negative.

A prime example is our home, which is *full* of unconscious anchors because we repeat so many patterns in familiar spaces.

For instance, you may walk into your favourite room and feel calm because it's where you relax. On the flip side, feeling tense when you enter the kitchen, because it's where arguments often happen, would indicate a negative anchor.

If you conk out on the couch right after work, it means that spot has become an anchor associated with sleep. When you climb into bed at night and get the urge to start a fight (perhaps that's what you and your partner usually do there), it means you've created a low-vibration conflict anchor to the bed.

Anchors can be a major issue because they hold us in a negative behavioural pattern or trigger trauma. Imagine what your unconscious self associates with your car if you feel embarrassed to drive it, or your work desk if you're dissatisfied with your job! Think about what kind of energy lingers in those spaces.

A few examples of my own anchors:

- Culture Club's song *Karma Chameleon* (1983) energises me, puts a smile on my face and leaves me in a happy state.
- The smell of freshly cut grass gives me feelings of love and comfort because of its association with my wonderful grandfather.
- Being called 'young lady' or called by my full name gives me anxiety, makes me feel like I'm in trouble and can even trigger a trauma response.

Thankfully, the anchors that don't serve us can be undone and reprogrammed. We simply need to *disrupt* the old pattern and create *new* conscious associations.

My son developed a negative association with our kitchen's island bench, which I had to work hard to undo.

Yes, it was my fault. Yes, I'm a very different mother today.

I was usually in the kitchen when my boys came home from school, and when my son appeared at the island bench, I'd bombard him with questions about his day: 'How was school? What'd you have for lunch? How'd you do on your test? Learn anything new today?' I never got a reply.

These days, I know why: I was overwhelming a child who was already overwhelmed by his day.

Over time, this repetition of bombardment developed into an anchor for my son that meant a trauma response and total shutdown. It became so cemented that, even when I asked him on a Sunday if he wanted his favourite food, he went silent and stared blankly through me.

What I didn't know back then is that males need about twenty minutes of decompression time between school or work and home; this is grounded in neuroscience and psychology (Gray, 1992). They need time to process the day's experiences and shift from the demands of the external world to the emotional and relational home environment. Basically, the male brain must close one box before it can open another.

As a woman, however, I sought connection and communication as soon as the men in my life were around, which is the opposite of what *they* needed.

Once I learned the distinction between *them* and *me*, I changed the routine and tried something new. I decided I wouldn't be in the kitchen at all when my son came home. Instead, when I heard him arrive, I'd call out from another room, 'Hi darling, I'll be out in twenty minutes.'

On weekends, I delivered *ridiculous* humour and fart noises to anyone who took a position at the kitchen's island bench.

I reworked the routine and reprogrammed the anchor. I elicited laughs, silliness and a sense of safety rather than interrogation and need.

Almost like magic, within a few weeks, my son became *completely* comfortable in the kitchen. Now, his anchor is one of positivity and peace.

We maintain the twenty-minute rule to this day.

Understanding anchors *is* this powerful! Once you spot them, you can change them. And when you do, you free yourself from reliving those old emotional reactions.

From the Case Files: Front Door Defence

A married couple came to me for help because the wife was triggered with intensely negative emotions whenever her husband arrived home from work.

Every day at 6 pm, as soon as she heard his key in the lock, her body would go rigid and feelings of anger would flood her. She stated there was no reason for her feelings, and nothing her husband said or did could calm her down.

'Can you imagine how he feels,' she said, 'coming home after a long day at work just to think he's already in trouble?'

I asked her to describe what happened at home every evening at 6 pm when she was between two and nine years old.

'Mum came home around that time. She was always tired and irritable from her job. She hated it. I wanted to sit with her and tell her about my day, but she went right into preparing dinner instead. She just couldn't ever relax, and it was my job to cheer her up so I could feel safe around her.'

I explained that the negative interactions with her mother had caused her to develop an anchor at a young age, and that her nervous system linked 6 pm with stress and a need to manage someone else's emotions. I described how her body was reliving this childhood experience every time she heard her husband's key in the door lock.

To disrupt the pattern, I first took her through my powerful Timeline Reset Process, and then formed a new plan for her to action upon her husband's arrival home from work.

She agreed to:

- meet him at the front door with it already open
- play happy, uplifting music while greeting him.

Thirty days later, the negative anchor was a thing of the past.

A new positive anchor had taken its place.

Today, the couple are thriving.

Self-Exploration: Revealing Your Anchors

Think about your day-to-day routines and the spaces you occupy.

Use the blank spaces below to describe any anchors you may have affecting your life.

Car:

Bedroom:

Living room:

Workspace:

Kitchen:

The Language Audit

What helps and what hinders?

Something we often take for granted is the freedom to express ourselves. It's a gift, but one we must be conscious of.

Why? Because words hold power. They're no different from our thoughts, feelings and actions.

Every word we utter exists on a vibrational level and carries an energetic agreement.

They also *transmute* energy, which is why we fuck things up for ourselves when we aren't present or aware of what we're saying. When we speak, the power our words hold shifts away from us. It's why we manifest what we say out loud rather than what we think.

Jason Parks summed this up beautifully when he said:

> *There's a very old teaching about energy dynamics and speaking things into reality. It is that words themselves are power itself. When they are contained within your mouth, you have the power. But when you speak it into the world, the world then holds the power* (Parks, 2024).

Wielding the power of words means we also need to place proper intention behind them. We need to start speaking what we want, instead of what we *don't*.

Remember the ancient pine analogy?

Well, our words should match the branch we wish to perch on. It means cutting 'ground-level' language and replacing it with positive, *uplifting* things that match the vibration of the 'treetop' instead.

The Fine Print of Self-Talk

The next time someone asks you how your day's going, take a pause and think about how you'd usually reply.

If it isn't something good, ask yourself *why?*

If it's something that sounds good, but you don't believe it's true, why not? What's stopping you from saying your day is amazing or excellent?

Sometimes, we default to negativity out of habit, not because our day is *actually* bad, but because we've conditioned ourselves to expect or highlight the worst. Does this sound like you?

Questioning the *reasons* behind our words does more than just help us use better language. It leads us to the reasons why our day feels subpar in the first place.

I once had a mouth abscess that persisted for nearly two weeks. Why? Because I was talking shit about myself without realising it, and my communicator body went into energetic warning mode. The abscess was like a neon sign that read: *You're shit-talking again!* Our body listens more than we think; it absorbs the energy of our words, turning internal shame into physical tension, stress and even pain.

So I immediately shifted my language to incorporate as *much* self-love as possible. It wasn't about pretending everything was perfect, but choosing to be kinder and more appreciative of myself despite the flaws I'd notice.

And that's the thing: what you say about yourself isn't who you are. At least, not until you speak it into reality.

So watch what you're saying to yourself. Be aware of the language you choose. When we're mean or cruel to ourselves, down toward the forest floor we plummet.

Rise *up* a few branches instead. Keep kindness and *good* intentions in your words. Speak to yourself and others with care and compassion.

Think about gossip for a moment. When we talk negatively about someone else, even if we think it's harmless, it plants a seed in our unconscious mind. Remember, our brain can't tell if we're talking about someone else or ourselves. Intention aside, we essentially sabotage our own well-being.

Over time, repetitive shit-talk can seep into how we see the world, judge others and even how we perceive ourselves. Since the words we use shape our reality, engaging in gossip trains our minds to pick out flaws. Yes, that can be flaws in others or our *own* mirror. It's a cycle that reinforces discontent and judgment, a space no one wants to exist in. Why? You guessed it: 'bottom-branch' living.

Now, let's change the fucking vibe!

Fuck, Love & Other Swears

If you think you can't hold an agreement on how a particular word can have an impact, think again. It's no accident this book is brimming with f-bombs and other so-called profanity. They're not just there to spice up your day. They're tools. Indicators. See, a word is *just* a word until there's an agreement or intention behind it. It's like the word below, which some people just can't say.

Me? I love it.

Graphic 8: Swears & Flowers

Look at it there, sitting on the page, doing *absolutely* nothing. Depending on the agreement you hold, that little four-letter wonder might have you laughing, flinching, rolling your eyes or clutching your pearls like you found it carved into a church pew.

I'm not in agreement with the vulgarity of *fuck*. My agreement is that when I use it, it holds actual value. It has density in *good* ways. It brings across a message.

And that's the differentiating factor: any agreements we hold with certain words will almost always be categorised as good or bad. There isn't really a neutral ground. Either it's acceptable to us, or it isn't.

It's also why some people struggle with the word *love* because love, like fuck, is loaded. Let me tell you, if you feel weird saying, 'I love you,' but you drop 'fuck' into casual conversation without a second thought, that's an agreement you maintain whether you realise it or not.

If the swearing in this book has a profound or substantial effect on you, ask yourself why. Where does that trigger come from? Who taught you to give those words such power, and why do you still hold that agreement today?

Better yet, would you like to reshape that agreement? Because you absolutely can. The only thing stopping you is the make-believe rulebook someone handed you once upon a time.

And if that book no longer serves you, then off it must fuck!

How Tiny Words Wreck Big Intentions

Before becoming a professional hypnotherapist, I was a stage hypnotist for comedy shows. It's incredible how much you can achieve in a performance with just words and skilful wordplay.

Take the word *try*, for example. Whenever you use it in your instructions to your hypnotised participants, anything you say afterwards gets cancelled out. You can order them to *try* picking something up, and they will *try*, but they won't succeed. They *literally* can't.

Now imagine someone saying to themselves, 'I'm gonna try to get the laundry done tomorrow.'

Red flag going up in your head? Good job! Because what have they just done? Cancelled out their intention with the word *try*. Their unconscious self doesn't process the negative term and, therefore, can't apply proper intention to the words that follow. It's safe to say the speaker won't complete the task they mentioned, as the outcome has already been determined by the words they chose to use.

We're either *doing* or we aren't. We either tell ourselves we'll accomplish things, or we won't. Trying is illusory, and once we understand that, it transforms into a choice we make.

Since the unconscious mind doesn't deal in negatives, what does that mean for our intentions in other areas of life? If I say, 'Don't think of a black cat,' what happens? Did your mind go right to a black cat? Now apply this to your everyday thoughts: *I won't get fat... I don't want to be broke... I can't find the time.* What part of these is your unconscious mind latching onto? *Fat. Broke. Can't.*

Imagine telling a restaurant server, 'No onions, please,' and getting a plate stacked with them.

Need I say more?

So ask yourself, 'Where's my *real* focus? What am I *actually* asking for? What am I *truly* saying?' If you think of your mind as a 'wish-granter', how would you phrase your requests to avoid black cats, no money and extra onions?

Here are some limiting words to avoid at *all* costs:

- try
- but
- can't
- don't
- won't

- unsure
- impossible
- redo
- recreate
- wish
- eventually
- later
- only.

Stop using these intention-shattering words. Swap in confident language and aim high rather than low. Reinforce your intention with your words and take advantage of the power you put out into the world with every single syllable.

Responding Instead of Reacting

How do we flip the script on negativity?

I ask so many of my clients and, just as often, myself this question: 'Which game are you choosing to play?' It's important to consider because it unveils yet another set of patterns we can change with SSPA.

You might be sick of hearing this by now, but it's worth repeating: *everything* is a frequency. The energy we engage with is a choice. How we react in any situation comes down to our agreements and identity.

And how are yours serving you?

Do they trigger an automatic reaction or a conscious response?

They may sound similar, but they're worlds apart.

Think about gaslighting, for example. If someone tries to gaslight us, we have two options: defend ourselves and get pulled into their game, or step back, recognise what's happening and choose a higher response. Instead of reacting, we can acknowledge the situation through a filter of compassion: *this person is hurting… they're in denial and protection mode.* We don't have to play the conflict game. Instead, we get the opportunity to go, 'What do you need right now?' or, 'What did I trigger in you that sparked the need to protect yourself?'

It's *our* choice.

By responding rather than reacting, we can disrupt the cycle. Pausing to consider more data uncovers previously hidden answers. So no more repetition. We empower ourselves when we respond in conscious ways, and every moment offers us that choice: reinforce the cycle or rise above it.

So choose wisely! Doing so unlocks better experiences for you, for them and for life.

Celebrating Every Achievement

Should that include the small stuff, too?

We rarely give ourselves enough credit. However, if we want to shift out of negativity, this *must* change.

Celebration is essential for long-term success. It helps us rewire our unconscious mind, teaching it to recognise that we are capable and retraining it to seek dopamine from joy rather than stress. We can say *adios* to cortisol.

So start celebrating yourself and your wins *every* damn time.

If you walk into the gym and only do one set, that still deserves a high-five.

If you make an *absolutely* perfect cup of tea, that's a victory.

If you don't burn the toast? You bet that's worth celebrating!

If you remember to take a deep breath before reacting to something stressful, or choose kindness over self-criticism, or catch yourself swapping a negative thought for something better, that's progress. You *deserve* to see it, feel it and honour it. No matter how small, it's the observable result of your positive actions.

As we train ourselves to acknowledge wins, we can choose how big our celebration will be. It doesn't have to be dramatic (unless that's your jam). Even a smile or a deep breath could work, or perhaps simply telling ourselves, 'Well done, me.' Every time we do this, we signal to our unconscious programs that we're all good and that it's safe to continue. Then, when we feel safe and good about what we're doing, it becomes easier to do more of it.

So from now on, no achievement will go unnoticed. Every step that doesn't take us backward is a worthy win. Every effort matters, and yes, that includes not burning the toast!

Set the Tone, Don't Fix the Mess

Have you ever eaten a big slice of cake, intending to walk it off later? When you start your day stressed and negative, do you tell yourself you'll shake the mood eventually? These approaches are reaction-driven, meaning they force you to compensate for something that has already happened.

Well, what if we flipped that on its head?

Instead of having to clean up after our choices, what if we adopted behaviours that meant we didn't have to clean up at all?

Changing your behaviour so you never have to 'clean up' is the difference between reactivity and proactivity, and it can apply to much more than exercise or mood.

Think big.

Think *every* thought and feeling we experience.

Consider proactivity the belle of your ball because it's a beautiful thing to incorporate into your way of life. Using it to become less reactive puts the power back in our hands. That, and it's just *easier*. Instead of waiting to 'walk off' an impulsive decision, what if we just avoided it in the first place?

Better yet, what if we applied this concept to situations of negativity and stress?

Making conscious choices about what we allow into our minds can look just like choosing to eat nourishing foods instead of things that leave us sluggish. It doesn't mean forcing ourselves to be happy, but pushing back against the thoughts and feelings that weigh us down.

We've all heard the phrase, 'Work smarter, not harder.' If you haven't, the principle is that we can accomplish more with *less* effort. It's something many people use in their work and home lives, yet they fail to apply it to their emotional and mental habits.

They're missing an enormous opportunity.

Think of your mind as a foundation: if you build it strong in the morning, you don't need to reinforce it throughout the day. Going into negativity means spending time and precious energy patching up cracks, so why not do it right the first chance you get?

Proactivity can also apply to the unconscious self.

When we get intentional about what we think and feel, we can steer clear of the things that make us twitch, as well as our unconscious programs that run on autopilot.

Being proactive means less fixing and more smooth sailing. It's our chance to get ahead of our patterns and behaviours, setting ourselves up for success before problems can even arise. Who wants to make decisions that they'll have to undo later, rather than ones they won't need to fix at all?

~ Bradley

Part Three

Success Strategies Workshop

Building Frameworks That Work For You

'Most folks are about as happy as they make up their minds to be.'
~ Abraham Lincoln

As soon as you trust yourself, you will know how to live.
~ Johann Wolfgang von Goethe

'If you must doubt something, doubt your limits.'
~ Price Pritchett

'Listen to the pain. It's both history teacher and fortune teller...
Sometimes, it's so bad, we feel like we're dying. But we can't really live
till we've died a little, can we?'
~ Blind Al, Deadpool

'Results are important, but the way they are achieved,
the process, is equally important.'
~ Robert Greene, The Laws of Human Nature

Chapter Eight

SSPA to the Next Level

Swap The 'Can't Do It' Mindset

It's January, and I'm in line for Doge's Palace in Venice, one of the most opulent places on Earth. The city's canals shimmer around me, and reedy notes of an accordion play, drifting on a salty breeze. My son takes in all the beauty while standing beside me.

And yet, despite the magical moment, up it rises, that familiar discomfort—a twinge of unease in the gut. Thoughts of work and lengthy to-do lists creep in, my responsibilities waiting for me when I return home.

I don't allow myself to linger in those thoughts for long. Why should I worry about February when I'm standing in the heart of Venice?

I smile.

My communicator body has just revealed a hidden belief lurking in my unconscious self. Something about happiness, and how much I'm *allowed* to receive before guilt and worry come to crash the party.

After a giant breath in, I think of SSPA. I picture my flamingo.

Only this time, she isn't alone. She's on one leg amongst a flock of gulls, balanced on a ruby gondola, precisely where my mind should be: in the present moment.

I look around and start naming things to anchor myself: carvings on the palace doors; the turquoise canal water; my son's bright eyes as he points at a passing yacht. As the tension melts away, I snap my fingers a few times and stand on one leg like my flamingo.

Just like that, the belief has lost its grip. The part of my unconscious mind that tells me to worry about the future instead of enjoying the present is gone. Just like that, I'm back in Venice with my son.

And my new belief? That happiness isn't something we need to earn. It's something we *allow* in.

~

So *is* SSPA quick and easy? Yes. Does it disrupt negative thought-emotion cycles? Yes. Does it plant good beliefs through intentional actions? One hundred per cent!

But SSPA can be *so* much more.

SSPA applies in long form just as effectively as short bursts, and I'll give you some custom hacks in this chapter.

But first…

Intention Matters

Are you a Roomba following a circuit?

Have you ever asked yourself if your momentum is stuck on a default setting? When a new client comes to me seeking help, the very first thing I ask them is, 'What have you tried before?'

It's a significant question because it gives me immediate insight into their journey so far.

If they advise they're new to this, I get excited and help them jump right in.

However, if they claim they've tried *everything* and nothing has worked for years, that's when I get concerned. It's a pretty big red flag and statistically improbable. If someone has tried counselling, psychiatry and psychology, it has to work to *some* degree.

My next question becomes, 'Do you practise what you learn between the sessions?' See, what we do in a session is exploration, finding a different way for them to think, feel and do. It's up to them to take action after they leave.

And that's usually the biggest issue. This work isn't an overnight thing. To build, we *must* practise what is new and do so with the intention of success.

Have Patience & Keep Going

How long until you see results?

Based on my clients' results, the average time before they see the benefits of their practise is three months. It means they do the work but may not reap the rewards for weeks. This can make it *so* challenging to persevere before the evidence shows. But I promise, as long as we act with intention and purpose, good manifestations will come.

Every thought, feeling, word and action is like writing a letter to the universe—one that takes three months to get back.

Today, that letter may look like falling in love with ourselves or growing our business.

Three months from now, we should be able to identify the tangible results of our efforts.

But what about all that time in between?

The time in between is where things can get tricky. This is where we need to get critical, looking back at what we thought, felt and acted on three months ago. The three-month time delay doesn't just apply to manifesting positive things, but *also* to negativity.

Think of it like this: we're still receiving what we thought, felt, spoke or acted on three months ago. It's important to think about the metaphorical letter we sent the universe back then, and what we indicated we wanted *more* of.

Let's say someone disrespected you.

Did you think about how bad it felt, or did you feel shame around the incident?

Did you speak ill of the person?

Did you go so far as to act like them and disrespect them back?

That's a letter signed, sealed and delivered, my friend. Worse, it's a magnetic energy that keeps you vibrating at the 'disrespect' frequency for the next several weeks.

Shit!

So how do you undo that? Through consistent, intentional action.

Going in the opposite direction is usually the most effective. You've got to counteract the disrespect by stopping your thoughts and feelings in their tracks and swapping in something like compassion. Get present with these new thoughts and feelings, and then take action to reinforce your change of heart.

Practising this for a few months gives your intention longevity.

With patience, your efforts will compound over time. That little seed of goodness will sprout a stem, which will turn into a trunk, and, eventually, branches.

Longevity and compounding are the long-game goals, as long as it's high-vibration goodness you're creating!

Now let's get to it.

Mashed Potato Composting

Can 'better' really grow from rot?

As far as the long-game stopping and swapping goes, this exercise is a favourite of mine. I love mashed potatoes, so why wouldn't I work them into my toolkit? Let's pretend your negative life events, stress and trauma are a big bowl of mashed potatoes sitting on the counter in front of you.

I don't know about you, but I like my potatoes best when they're fresh and hot. I'd settle for the ones from yesterday, but not much older than that. I probably wouldn't eat last week's, and wouldn't even touch last month's. Would you? How about mashed potatoes from an entire *year* ago? I think not! They'd be nasty—some *really* gross shit.

Now imagine taking a good look inside that bowl. How old are those mashed potatoes in relation to the problems they represent? Twenty years? Thirty years? What do potatoes that old even look like? Smell like? Taste like? Whatever state they're in, it won't be good.

Why, then, are you still chowing down on those nasty potatoes? It's because you've developed a habit of sprinkling fresh goodness on top. That way, you can stomach all the mould and decay hidden underneath.

But, unfortunately, that doesn't work for long. Fresh ingredients just become mould on top of mould.

Get introspective instead. Ask yourself what's lingering in your potatoes. What goodness did you sprinkle on them that has also soured? What agreements have you mixed into the mess that might shape negative identities within you?

Okay. Time to ditch those *nasty* potatoes.

But wait, don't just dump them in the bin!

Sure, the stench might dissipate once you've thrown them out, but you'll still be sitting in that 'gross potato' vibration. Sure, throwing them out might make life simpler, but then you'd miss the opportunity to turn shit into gold.

No, the perfect place for your old mashed potatoes is on the metaphorical compost pile.

So get dumping! Imagine going out into the garden and throwing them right on top of that pile. Scrape your bowl clean with a spatula, even.

Now you'll leave it for the worms. Walk away, knowing innately that something beautiful will soon grow from the disaster. Trust that when you return in a few months, new life will have sprouted, and it will be something beautiful and better than before.

Conversion is key with this exercise. We *want* to transform our potatoes, because as we do, we transmute the energy associated with their represented negativity, and we look at our past in a new way. We start setting up our future instead of feeling helpless because of the past. Everything ebbs and flows. Water cannot remain stagnant with things moving and growing in it; what we think is stagnant is still *active*.

And that's our trauma. That's our shame, guilt, hopelessness, negativity, stress and limiting belief systems. Those old mashed potatoes still need to move, to be transmuted.

Let's face it: if we're coming from *shit*, we're going to get more *shit*.

But if we come from a place of growth instead, we'll end up creating awesomeness.

SSPA Exercise: Composting

What could happen if you converted your old, mouldy mashed potatoes? What might grow from the decay? Choose some 'potatoes' you'd like to put into the compost and begin growing them into something beautiful.

Take a few minutes to answer or sketch about the following questions.

What do my 'old potatoes' and persisting problems say about me?

What problems do these beliefs cause?

What am I not realising about myself because of my 'old potatoes'?

What am I going to do with my 'old potatoes' and persisting problems?

Am I ready to dump them for good? Why?

Who am I after 'composting' my 'old potatoes'? What are my new feelings and perspectives?

What kind of joy and excitement does my new identity bring?

What do I see/realise about myself now?

Is the growth working for or against me? Why?

How do I feel about my future now?

Fairytales Can Come True

What if you could re-tell the story?

This process is so simple that there's only one rule: always think, write or speak from a place of positivity.

Don't forget, words hold vibration. They wield power and help magnetise things toward us. Therefore, when something comes up that really troubles us (a thought, feeling, situation or identity), the worst thing we can do is sit in its low-vibration energy and give it mass.

Instead, we can create a *new* story, telling ourselves this fairytale version and determining the happy outcome we want.

Put some quick distance between you and a shitty thought or feeling by reframing it. If you imagine your fairytale is a spell (if you write yours down, then it absolutely *is* a spell), do you want it to harm you or help you? You won't get any help from negativity, so don't go there. The more feel-good, the better.

Imagine you're looking in a mirror, overtaken by feelings of dissatisfaction.

Catch yourself and stop.

Swap the thought for something like this:

- 'I love that I get to heal my body.'
- 'I love my body and am happy choosing self-love every day.'
- 'I have the most amazing eyes/smile/curves/angles/complexion.'
- 'I love that I'm beautifully unique/uniquely beautiful.'

What we *don't* want to do is this:

- 'I *really* want to stop hating my body.'
- 'I'm not the most beautiful, but I'm alright.'
- 'I *actually* don't care what I look like.'
- 'One day I won't be so dissatisfied.'

We don't want to release the energy of 'dissatisfied', 'hating' and 'don't care' into the universe. Avoid attaching these negative and low-vibration words to yourself and your body.

Change the *entire* programmed response.

You'll be glad you did!

SSPA Exercise: Script Your New Narrative

Story time!

Record an overarching truth about yourself so you can transmute the thoughts into words. Fill in the blanks as you reflect on a part of your life you don't view as 'good', adopting a new agreement around it as you go.

NB: If you need help join our Stop It Swap It - Official Readers Group @ https://www.facebook.com/groups/stopitswapit/.

Tip: Bookmark this page to remind yourself of the agreement you now embody.

Once upon a time, _________________*(name)* felt like a total

_________________*(adjective)*.

_________________*(name)* believed that

_________________________________*(statement about self)*

and ___________________________________*(statement about life)*.

Every day used to be _________________*(adjective)* because of these beliefs.

Then one day, _________________*(name)* realised the truth: they were actually _________________*(adjective)* and _________________ *(adjective)*.

And because of that, ___________________________________ *(statement about what's changed)*.

And because of *that*, ___________________________________ *(statement about new abundances)*.

Until finally, __________________*(name)* could admit:

____

(statement about self-love).

Ever since that day, _______________*(name)* felt like a brilliant and undeniable _______________*(adjective).*

Elevate by Ditching Resentment

Is there anything more powerful than peace?

To understand resentment, we first need to clarify our understanding of anger. When we suffer an injury or insult to our soul, anger flares. It's hot and intense, but very clean. Healthy anger—not to be confused with violence, which is *usually* unhealthy—burns off negativity and diminishes, leaving us with space. It's our spirit awakening to push out that *shitty* energy so we can move forward with a cheerful soul.

This kind of anger is beneficial for us when it functions as intended. It's when we suppress it, however, that it turns into resentment.

Resentment is like a slow poison that seeps through us, often without us even realising. It affects us on all levels, keeping us rooted in the past and reliving old wounds we refuse to release, which makes it impossible for us to move forward. We become blind to the present and new opportunities to heal and grow.

This kind of energy vampire is a heavy sucker. It lowers our vibration and prevents us from aligning with those upper frequencies of love, peace and abundance. And our connection to Source? Forget it.

Resentment fucks with our ability to access our higher self and the flow of good energy. It kills off our chances for growth.

Much like trauma, resentment can manifest in the body, causing it to respond with tension, stress or even illness (Rose, 2013). Think of consequences like chronic pain, fatigue, digestive issues and degenerative disease.

When I say it's nasty, I mean *nasty*.

The only permanent way to reclaim our power is to release resentment. We just have to let go. This *usually* involves releasing any attachment to the offender and the offences against us—tough, but doable. Then, as we sit with it and embrace the intention to release, we'll feel it go.

It can be both weird and beautiful when it does. As the heart expands and our intercostal spaces relax, we tend to feel lighter, like we've just exhaled or sighed deeply.

That's our cue to release the resentment we hold toward *ourselves* around the offence.

Let's be clear: letting go does *not* mean we're condoning what happened. It just means we're no longer willing to let it control us.

Only then can we regain power and allow energy to flow freely again.

SSPA Exercise: Prayer for Release

I use the prayer below if I'm struggling to let go of deep feelings, especially around an offence or offender. Take a moment to ponder where you have an instance of resentment, then set your intention to let go and speak this out loud:

> *Beloved Source,*
>
> *I lay down all resentment now, gently and completely.*
>
> *I no longer carry what was never meant to live in my heart.*
>
> *I wrap myself in compassion for every way I learned to survive.*
>
> *I forgive myself. I soften toward myself. I return to love.*
>
> *I receive the healing already unfolding.*
>
> *I trust in the restoration already taking place.*
>
> *I thank you for the peace that is now reclaiming me.*

Return to these words whenever your heart feels weighed down or constricted. They are a pathway back to softness.

You can use the space below to create your own prayer for release:

From 'Fuck You' to 'Thank You'

Where can you shift resentment to gratitude?

My husband and I sat across from each other, both holding pens. Minds on edge. Hesitant.

We weren't about to write just any old letter; this would be the most brutally honest, no-filter thing we'd ever put to paper.

A *fuck you* letter.

The rules were simple: every sentence had to start with *Fuck you*, and our words had to be pure emotion. There could be no softening of edges, no excuses and no pretending we were above our anger.

These letters would be the raw, ugly truth: *Fuck you for not being there for me… Fuck you for making me feel small… Fuck you for leaving me to deal with it alone.*

Our pens ripped into the paper.

Our tears smudged the ink.

We let it all out in five minutes, without holding back a single bit of resentment, frustration or pain. And then, without rereading or second-guessing, we tore our letters to pieces.

Outside, we burnt the tatters to ash and transmuted our thoughts to oblivion.

Something shifted then. The weight seemed lighter. Gone, even. In its place rose a surprising new thought: *Thank you.*

So, we went back inside and wrote again.

This time, our letters came out differently: *Thank you for trying, even when you didn't know how… Thank you for teaching me resilience… Thank you for being part of my journey.*

That night, I looked at my husband in a new way. Not from the perspective of old wounds, but through a softer lens.

Great healing comes from acknowledging anger and pain, then choosing to let it go. Pushing these things away only makes them worse.

That, or they turn into resentment.

So don't hold on. Instead, use this method to gain freedom.

155

SSPA Exercise: The Two Letters

Pretending we were never hurt doesn't heal us. Instead, we must transform that pain into something new.

So let's do it!

1. Get some shit off your chest: take five to ten minutes to write a *fuck you* letter to a person, thing or situation. Be raw and real.
2. Transmute that old, shitty energy: rip up or safely burn the letter. Let those thoughts die with it.
3. Find new gratitude to replace the shit: write a *thank-you* letter instead. Make it honest and personal.
4. Keep it close: store the letter somewhere you can revisit when you need a reminder of your own growth.

SSPA Exercise: Letters to Yourself

Use the exercise above for deep and real introspection by focusing on *yourself,* and write three short sentences for each letter in the space below.

Positive Affirming Prayer

What do you need to speak into existence?

Following SSPA, the next quickest way to find ease is through prayer (no, I'm not talking about reciting a dozen 'Hail Marys' or half the Bible).

But before we get into all of that, it would be good to define what prayer *actually* is. In essence, any communication of gratitude, surrender or request from your spirit to another is a prayer.

Pretty simple, right?

Remember: just like how our words carry vibration, mass and power, so do our thoughts.

Through influencers like organised religion, textbooks, inspirational journals and family traditions, we're led to believe that prayers must follow certain structures, complexities and even themes.

This isn't true. Prayers are created and driven by the individual who is thinking or saying them. They can be as formal, informal, elaborate or abrupt as the reciter wishes.

What matters is the *intention* behind the words. When we think or speak with prayerful conviction and genuineness, it can shift us out of a terrible place and into a better vibration.

Prayer can be a highly useful tool when we're experiencing doubt, weakness, shame, fear, self-doubt, upset or general discomfort. Not only does it align our thoughts with positivity, but it also opens up a stronger connection to Source.

Some simple examples are:

- 'Flood me with ease and health in this moment.'
- 'Thank you for this beautiful sunrise and amazing fresh air.'
- 'I release all thoughts and feelings not serving me.'
- 'My puppies are wonderful, and I love them *so* fucking much.'

Gratitude is a highly efficient way to raise vibration. It can be gratitude for the trees and flowers, your significant other, a recent promotion or life upgrade, adorable kittens, baby sloths or anything else that brings you joy.

Developing a simple-to-recall prayer means you don't have to think too hard to make it happen. Think of something you can memorise, store on your phone or spell on a small paper tucked in your wallet.

Then, simply fill your thoughts with it when you need it, pop a smile on your face, and let the feeling of puppies or baby sloths flood through you.

Let's not kid ourselves, though: if shit has hit the fan and you're in a pit of despair, it will be impossible to find gratitude for the issue at hand. There is never a solution *in* the problem, so we don't need to look there.

SSPA Exercise: Personal Prayers

Take five to ten minutes and create a prayer list you can work into your daily routine.

Use the following prompts to create your own single-sentence prayers. Look at replacing any negatives with quick new positives.

Tip: The more your affirmations apply to specific negative self-beliefs, the better.

Thank you for _________________________________.

I release ______________ *and ask for* ______________ *in its* *place.*

Flood ______________ *with love, light and health.*

Help ______________ *overcome* ______________________

Space Embrace

We fall, as Emma likes to say, 'back into the shit' when we don't realise how much weight we're lugging around.

I'm not talking about physical weight; rather, the emotional and energetic burdens we've grown accustomed to. All the *stuff* our unconscious mind has clung onto because of shame, trauma, agreements and identity—our clutter.

I learned through no small feat that getting myself out of the metaphorical basement of vibration definitely isn't where the work stops. We also have to keep ourselves from backsliding.

Ironically, the way we hold on to physical things looks similar to how we store our internal clutter. Hoarding isn't always overflowing closets or jam-packed storage units. Often, the physical stuff is a representation of our emotional, mental or energetic hoarding. And, like physical things, the accumulation of *internal* things can happen without us even noticing.

No matter what form, holding on to old things and past agreements keeps us trapped.

We might hold on to objects that belonged to past versions of ourselves to keep those versions alive, even weakly. We may cling to beliefs that keep us stuck, stories about who we are that aren't true, or limitations on what we think we deserve from the universe. We carry around past pain as though it's still a vital part of our identity because letting go might mean discrediting our struggles.

Whatever the case, there's an overarching truth no one can escape: our environment reflects our energy.

When we surround ourselves with old, stagnant *stuff* that's doing nothing but collecting dust, we vibrate at the same low frequency. As the stacks grow taller, low-vibration energy multiplies, and we find comfort in the chaos—our energy syncs.

Mess becomes normal.

The same thing happens to us internally.

When old patterns and programs fill our minds, where do we find room for fresh ideas?

How can joy and love possibly live in a heart already bursting with unresolved grief?

If we're always in the company of people who exploit and exhaust our energy, how do we maintain the capacity to discover better companions?

Ever wonder why it can feel so fucking good to clear out a room? It's because the relief has more to do with shifting energy than it does with cleanliness. When we donate clothes, empty drawers or throw out broken things, we elevate. Our actions *literally* make space for new possibilities. And that happens on all levels.

It's not magic, but it sure can feel like it!

If this is resonating, ask yourself these questions:

- What am I holding onto that's keeping me from getting out of the shit?
- What can I let go of physically, mentally and emotionally?
- What action might lighten my load?

Avoiding the backslide means letting go, not pushing forward. The more stagnation and weighty energy you can ditch, the easier it will get to climb.

~ Bradley

Chapter Nine

Your Identity: New Management

You're Custom-Built, Not A Factory Model

Building something new is like planting a seed that will soon grow into a whole tree. Where is your tree growing? What does it look and feel like? Is it growing flowers or fruit? What challenges stand in the way of its growth? What *compost* will you use to help it flourish?

Don't forget, the reason we're here on earth is to heal and elevate. But it's up to us to look at where our progress is stalling. What's stopping us from thriving in positivity and success? What wounds are in our way? What can we release to make room for building something new?

But if we want to build, we first have to release. They go hand-in-hand. It's why we venture within, have a good look around and think: *Oh, I need to heal that.* Healing and releasing gives us space to *want* something, and that fuels our motivation to build.

Building is a critical part of life. Guess what happens when we stop? We slip into depression. We end up spiralling because we've got no hope for the future.

When we aren't creating or building, we're collapsing.

So release to create. You already have a reason, and it's the same one that compelled you to read this book.

I've said it a few times, and I'll say it again: change is practise, practise, practise. It can be tough, but I cannot emphasise enough how important it is to give yourself permission to *try*.

Allow yourself to embrace those messages from your communicator body. Throw out those old programs as you unearth them. Just get rid of them. The power to improve our circumstances sits within us; we just have to trust ourselves to get there.

Think, Feel, Say, Do

Are your misaligned behaviours costing you?

Rather than appearing out of nowhere, negativity follows a pattern or path. Each step on this path reinforces the next, gaining momentum, until the cycle becomes our reality. Good thing we can disrupt the process before it takes hold!

We have four key moments to stop negativity from becoming an act that we regret or a belief that shapes part of our identity.

It can start with a thought.

Perhaps we criticise ourselves, doubt our abilities or pass judgment on a situation. If we don't catch it, it moves into a feeling, influencing our emotions, energy and hormones.

From there, it can seep into what we say, whether through self-talk or when we speak to others. Finally, it manifests in our actions and choices, in what we do.

Each stage carries more weight than the one before. Our thoughts are the easiest to adjust, but once negativity has moved into our emotions, it becomes harder to shake. If it infiltrates our words, we start giving it power. By the time it turns into action, that's it. It's a done deal, and one that's pretty hard to undo.

Recognising when these moments are occurring means we can seize the chance to SSPA before negativity takes root. Catching it early is *so* important.

Of course, knowing the theory is one thing. But how does it look in real life?

Here's what it looked like for me.

My son and I were in London, visiting family we'd left behind when I moved us back to Australia. We'd planned a reunion, but on the day, my ex-husband and his family stood us up.

It hurt me, but it *devastated* my son. As he broke down next to me, I went straight into vengeance mode. I was busy concocting a plan to drive out to my ex's place, scale the house like a ninja, and raise holy hell when I started to wonder why I'd been so triggered so fast.

The quick answer is that I wanted to make the situation more bearable for my son.

Why? Because I was in a world of shame: *Why did I ever marry that dickhead, and what the fuck made me stay for seven years?* Inside, my communicator body was screaming. Outside, I was making things about me.

Once I realised what was going on, it clicked: I was in a trauma response myself. I wanted to fight the bastard who hurt my son. Mumma Bear was out for blood and dangerously close to slipping into a bottom-rung vibrational level.

Now, if I'd said or done anything from there, that would've been game over. But I didn't follow through.

Sure, I thought about it. And boy did I *feel* it!

But since I didn't respond or do anything, I never completed the process.

Thank *fuck* I could SSPA and reverse out of it.

As I stopped my thoughts, I focused on my son instead. I swapped that feeling of pure rage for my flamingo and used my son as a way to ground myself in the present moment.

And my unexpected action? Staying right where I was.

It tore me up to have my adult son sob on me, let go and talk about how hard that rejection was to take. But I had to just sit there. I couldn't make this about me.

Sometimes, the best thing we can do is to do nothing. Just shut up. We don't lessen it for our children, but let them have their moment.

So I did. I held my son like he was a baby, because it was the child in him that was hurting. It wasn't the twenty-two-year-old man, but the little boy that he had reverted to when the grief and pain of rejection came up.

And that rejected little boy needed safety, not a lioness.

Better Consistency, Better Outcomes

What habits could change your life?

Real trauma is tangible and 'in the moment'. It's someone coming at us with a weapon, or the driver who's lost control of their car.

But lingering trauma isn't *today's* reality, so let's stop playing its cyclical game. Otherwise, nothing changes. We *stay* in negativity. We *stay* in shame. And what does shame lead to? You got it: avoidance, denial and a plethora of coping mechanisms. We reach for wine, junk food, the latest show to binge on, whatever shifts our energy and keeps us from our responsibility.

Once again, the challenge is in the questions we ask ourselves:

- What am I not doing that I know will foster the change I seek?
- What action might I be avoiding that could change everything?
- How can it be applied to my relationships, business or personal life?
- What conversation, commitment or truth am I dodging?

I ask these questions almost daily. Do I always act on them? No, but I'm consistently working on them. Growing and healing are processes, and the more we take back control of our own energy, the easier we dispel old cycles.

~

Let's get super-serious for a minute and talk about something you'll be hard-pressed to find in textbooks: the big *why* question.

People are always searching for it; they always want to know. *Why do I feel like this? Where did it come from?* We search for some big revelation that will explain the origin of our struggles.

But through my research and repeated personal discoveries, I've realised that the question of *why* is often an excuse we hide underneath self-reflection. It keeps us in a sort of limbo, sailing the same waters, waiting for the clouds to part before we take action. The *why* then becomes our scapegoat, our reason for all the ongoing 'stuckness'.

After a challenging round of introspection, I discovered that I wanted to know more about a personal matter. As soon as I asked myself *why*, my mind drew forth the most convenient excuse it could: *Mum*. She didn't deserve to be blamed, but it was easier to blame her than take responsibility for my *own* responses. I thought I was searching for answers, but really, I was looking for someone to pin it all on.

And to be honest, I needed to grow the fuck up.

We humans are prone to falling into patterns and then acting like we have no control over them. *I can't help it. It's how I've always been. It's just how my brain works.* Pretending like 'always' is a valid reason to keep doing the same dumb thing over and over again is nothing but a trap.

We need to get real with ourselves if we want to achieve lasting change. It's time to shift from consistently blaming to *consistently* working through things in order to come out the other side better. We must ask ourselves: At what point do we throw our hands up? When do we stop letting old wounds shape our present? When do we decide not to continue behaviours and habits we aren't proud of?

Change is hard, and I won't ever deny that, but it's also not that complicated. If we don't like a pattern, we *can* stop doing it. Try something different. Something new. Replace a bad habit with a better one. Practise all those good consistencies to make them easier and easier.

Sometimes, it's about small, deliberate choices rather than big, dramatic transformations. Conscious action moves us closer to the person we truly want to be. It isn't about being perfect, but instead, it's about moving in the right direction and being consistent.

So if you're prone to reacting defensively, practise pausing.

If you default to self-doubt, practise self-trust.

If you shut down or withdraw during discomfort, practise staying open.

If you find yourself stuck in *why* all the time, practise asking yourself, *What now?* instead.

When we apply consistent and intentional effort to our problems, that's when everything shifts.

Compounding that Works for You

The bank account analogy

Each time we think, feel, say or do something, we're investing in our energy and vibrational levels. Think of it like banks and deposits. Suppose you've got two bank accounts: one at the Bank of Awesome and another at the Bank of Shame. Empowered choices equal a deposit into the Bank of Awesome, while things like self-doubt, negativity and victimhood mean a deposit into the Bank of Shame.

Which bank do you want holding your energetic investment?

It's critical to remember that your balance at either bank depends on what you continuously put in. You can't escape the math: small deposits made over time compound into something massive, whether we realise it or not. When we're in a cycle of feeling like crap, guess what's happening behind the scenes? Compounding. When we feel broke, there's a solid chance we've been making investments in lack, scarcity and frustration and depositing into the Bank of Shame.

Now, this system doesn't care if we use it for greatness or destruction. It simply follows the deposits we make and influences the direction we're headed, meaning it's a program we can change. We can use the compounding effect to work *for* us rather than against us. It just boils down to compounding consistently in good ways. But what if what you're doing isn't working? Change.

And if that doesn't seem to work? Change again.

Keep moving. Keep adjusting. It's okay to pivot. You can evolve because you aren't a static being. In fact, it's *necessary* to change and evolve, but ensure you're making deposits that serve you. Invest in the Bank of Awesome and let compounding work to your advantage.

And if you ever feel like it's not? Change. Believe me, we're built for it!

Failing Forward Without Shame

Do you see failure as proof you're still in the game?

The SSPA recipe helps you achieve change more easily, full stop. When people say, 'Oh, cool, the ingredients are right here. I'm going to cook with them right *now*,' they're getting it. They're implementing action that affirms their intention.

But let's be honest: sometimes, they'll burn the meal. Other times, it might end up raw. Perhaps they'll add too much of one thing and not enough of another, all of which is okay! It's part of practising, and ultimately, they'll nail it.

Once they've learned and accepted that nothing, and I mean *nothing*, is because of someone else, the recipe almost makes itself.

See, it doesn't matter how a situation has ended up or how someone has treated us. And while the actual event may not be our fault, how we handle our lives from then on is *absolutely* our responsibility.

We have to stop behaving in shame-based, blaming ways if we want to rise to higher vibrational levels and leave the shit behind. We do so much damage when we seek help and only end up proving to ourselves that we're still victims and disempowered. And by now, we know all that damage leads us straight into feelings of failure and shame.

I want to be *so* clear about something: failure is one of the greatest gifts we receive in life. It occurs naturally as we learn new things; it isn't something to fear. It provides us with invaluable contrast.

The real key is in *how* you choose to fail.

Failure is okay, as long as you're failing forward and not backward.

Failing backward is the act of trying something once or twice and then stopping. It's what happens when we let our thoughts and feelings sabotage our learning process. We end up saying, 'I'm never doing *that* again!' Whereas, failing forward is the act of continuing to try. It's brushing yourself off and working out a different way, reworking how you prep the ingredients for your metaphorical recipe.

So are you willing to turn on the stovetop and get cooking?

Self-Exploration: A Reimagined Future

Take five to ten minutes to journal about these questions:

What does a 'new normal' look like for me?

How does it help me to avoid negativity or slipping back down the branches of vibration?

Who do I want to be?

Who inspires me to be better than before?

What do I deserve from a 'new normal'?

How can I achieve it?

Is It Easier to Sink or Swim?

I think the answer is pretty easy: swim, of course.

When my son and I got back from our challenging month in Europe, my head was spinning. I couldn't comprehend what we'd just been through.

I admitted to my son that I was struggling to work it all out.

He turned to me and said, 'You don't *need* to work it out. Your spirit knows what happened. Your soul knows what happened. Your energy and body know what happened. If you're trying to theorise stuff, you're gonna fuck it up.'

I love my kids!

I bring this up to remind you not to add stones to your own pockets. Grow feathers. Detach from doubt and elevate yourself. With consistency, you can soar. You can magnetise everything good instead of what lives in low vibrations. You can rise into acceptance of self, put your soul back in charge and let your communicator body take a well-earned break.

Give yourself permission to stop those *well, fuck* moments and swap them for *ahh, that's nice*. Take it one altered thought at a time. It's so doable, and it gets more effective over time.

If you find it hard to look at yourself in the mirror like I used to, then stand there anyway. Remind yourself that you're beautiful and amazing, flaws and all. Give the most love and density to the part you like least.

Then, apply this to your career.

After that, do it with your finances.

As you become comfortable with SSPA and the resulting changes, apply it to your entire life. Be proud of everything you achieve!

You are so fucking important, Darling Heart.

You just have to believe it.

Creating in Surrender, Not Control

I used to maintain a chokehold on everything I created in my life. I began projects with a clear objective and subjected myself to immense pressure, driven by a desperation to see my work and efforts yield external value, such as financial rewards. An old belief system urged me to create *only* if it achieved something and *only* if that achievement fit the image in my mind. The specific outcome shaped everything I did as I worked toward that goal.

Some might call this the act of manifesting, but there's a huge difference between *driving* the outcome and envisioning possibilities. What I did was the former, and it was all based on control.

Imagine you're staring at a painting; you're so close to it that your nose nearly touches the canvas.

What do you see?

Odds are it's nothing but a blotchy patchwork of brushstrokes and shapeless forms. You know the painting extends the length of the room, but that kind of scale is too great to observe from where you're standing.

A friend tells you about a beautiful rose garden painted at the other end, but it might as well be invisible. The entire piece is just *too* big. You're too busy with the tiny section in front of you, and frankly, you're comfortable here. You know exactly what you're getting.

We tend to do the same with the outcomes we attach to creating. Knowing where we're going and what to expect when we get there equates to safety for our unconscious programs and a sense of control for our conscious mind.

However, we overlook the possibility that our desired outcomes may not align with those Source has designed for us. Perhaps they're supposed to be even *better*—but poor us, we've left no other doors open for opportunity. That better outcome isn't possible because we've *actually* blocked it by maintaining a small-picture mentality.

What if we surrendered instead?

It's time to step back from that painting and get the bigger picture.

Surrender is often deeply misunderstood. Most people would think of surrender in the context of a war, which is a fitting metaphor for what we're about to look at, because the opposite of surrender is control, aggression, steering, inflexibility and, in some cases, even theft.

For me, surrender is trust. It's the act of opening those doors we hold shut because they don't align with our vision of the outcome or the future. Surrender is a wormhole to more chances and possibilities in life. We may dictate direction, but we don't govern the design.

Think back to the TV channel analogy.

Are we the network producer or the channel viewer? I keep as many doors of opportunity open as I possibly can, hoping that in doing so, I allow every possibility for Source's design to lead me to the outcome meant for me, not what I had firmly planted in my mind.

Being an author has always been a dream of mine, but I never envisioned it through self-help or non-fiction. I have half a dozen fiction manuscripts in progress, yet those weren't the books that led me into authorship.

It was SSPA. It was what you now hold your hands.

This book wasn't part of my plan, yet it has proven fulfilling, motivating and worth every ounce of time taken to write, edit and polish it into what it is now. The result has been greatly rewarding and serves a purpose that surpasses my other writing projects.

And it was nowhere on my radar of 'things Bradley will do as an author'.

I'm as proud of SSPA as I am of my fiction work. That said, the role my fiction manuscripts play in the greater design is unknown to me. And that's okay, because my identity is no longer one of control, but surrender. I envision my future accomplishments, but I don't *command* the pathway toward them. Instead, I sit back and enjoy the ride, wherever it may lead.

This also applies to our healing journeys. And with tools like SSPA, moving forward in a positive direction has never been so maintainable. It's okay *not* to know where we're headed. Sometimes, that's part of the design.

Every step we take into the unknown is an act of courage, signalling to the universe that we are living in trust and openness.

We aren't meant to paint the greater picture alone, so put control aside and walk confidently forward. Trusting the design can transform you into who you were always meant to be.

Embrace it.

You've got this.

~ Bradley

Apply SSPA in 20 Life Domains

Remember:

- Your thoughts can create bad feelings that trigger an associated negative hormone, which often leads to a trauma response.
- A thought about the past or future is *not* your current reality; you're in control.
- If you end up in a trauma response, give your body ninety seconds to flush out the associated hormone. Don't stay in the negativity because it'll keep the hormone cycling through your system on repeat.

SSPA takes practise and time to get right. Along the way, ensure you're congratulating yourself for giving it a red-hot go!

Career

Without SSPA: We can spiral into self-doubt, which leads to procrastination, lack of confidence and missed opportunities. It can make us feel small, or it can cause our actions to become large and distorted. It can make us the life of the party and constantly seek validation.

With SSPA: We rewire our mindset for success, take action and build confidence.

Benefits: Increased productivity, resilience and career growth, which can lead to more money. It brings a sense of accomplishment and pride.

Overcoming Self-Doubt at Work

Thought: *I'm not good enough for this role.*

Stop: Recognise the thought and shut it down before it spirals.

Swap: Picture a flamingo dancing on one leg.

Get Present: Take three deep breaths, ground yourself and look around. Name five things or more.

Action: Focus on one small task you know you can do well right now. This will prove to your caudate nucleus that you are better than your negative thoughts.

Dealing with a Difficult Boss

Thought: *They always criticise me.*

Stop: Recognise the thought and shut it down before it spirals.

Swap: Picture a goldfish blowing rainbow bubbles.

Get Present: Focus on what is in front of you: five to ten things.

Action: Say into the mirror, '[your name], you *are* amazing.' In more serious situations, begin searching for another job where you'll be treated better.

Contribution & Giving

Without SSPA: Doubting your impact discourages you from helping others.

With SSPA: You recognise your value and give freely. Then, under the Universal Law of Tithing, the universe will give back to you threefold.

Benefit: A greater sense of purpose, fulfilment and connection.

Fear of Speaking Up in Meetings

Thought: *What if I sound stupid?*

Stop: Recognise the fear before it silences you.

Swap: Imagine a turtle with a microphone.

Get Present: Feel your feet on the ground and the chair supporting your back.

Action: Speak up at least once in the meeting.

Tip: it doesn't have to be more than a few seconds.

Creativity

Without SSPA: Fear of failure blocks creative flow.

With SSPA: You trust the process and express yourself freely.

Benefit: More inspiration, joy and artistic confidence.

Letting Go of Perfectionism

Thought: *If I can't do it perfectly, I shouldn't do it at all.*

Stop: Notice the all-or-nothing thinking before it holds you back.

Swap: Picture a joyful puppy running in circles.

Get Present: Look around and name five to ten things; whatever gets you back into the now. Avoid creating a reality out of the past or future by continuing in the same thought pattern.

Action: Set a timer for ten minutes and create without judgment. Let go of the outcome and focus on enjoying the process.

Education

Without SSPA: Fear of failure blocks learning potential.

With SSPA: You stay open and engaged in the learning process.

Benefit: Faster learning, retention and personal growth.

Feeling Overwhelmed by Homework

Thought: *There's too much to do.*

Stop: Pause before the stress becomes paralysing.

Swap: Imagine a purple llama in a party hat.

Get Present: Focus on your breath. Breathe in for the count of four, hold for four and breathe out for four. Do this four times.

Action: Break tasks into fifteen minute chunks and tackle one piece at a time in order to build momentum.

Environment

Without SSPA: Feeling overwhelmed by clutter leads to inaction.

With SSPA: You shift into control and take small, effective steps.

Benefit: A peaceful, organised space that supports your well-being.

Improving Sleep

Thought: *I can't stop my mind from racing.*

Stop: Acknowledge the chaos before it overwhelms you or leads to anxiousness.

Swap: Imagine a baby panda snuggling in a blanket.

Get Present: Focus on your breath, counting each inhale, and exhale slowly.

Action: Create a bedtime routine that signals your brain it's time to rest. Dim lights, stretch gently or journal your thoughts.

Family & Parenting

Without SSPA: Old patterns and triggers create ongoing family tension.

With SSPA: You break cycles, respond consciously and foster love.

Benefit: Healthier family dynamics, deeper understanding and peace.

Staying Patient with Your Child

Thought: *My child is so difficult.*

Stop: Notice the frustration rising before it gets intense.

Swap: Picture a squirrel holding a tiny acorn.

Get Present: Take a deep breath and relax your body, feel your feet on the ground and bring yourself back to your body.

Action: Pause before reacting, then choose a response that aligns with the calm parent you want to be. Smile. Come from a place of love instead of frustration; it will stop your child's state of fear.

Letting Go of Parenting Guilt

Thought: *I'm not a good enough parent.*

Stop: Catch the self-criticism before it takes over and becomes a feeling with hormonal attachment.

Swap: Imagine a sparkly polar bear hugging its cub.

Get Present: You know what to do! Look around and name five to ten things. Keep going until you're completely back in the present moment.

Action: Practise self-compassion by reciting the affirmation, 'Every day, in every way, I'm getting better and better.'

Handling Tantrums Calmly

Thought: *My child is out of control.*

Stop: Notice your frustration before it escalates.

Swap: Picture a baby zebra prancing playfully.

Get Present: Take a deep breath and ground yourself.

Action: Get down to your child's level. Open your arms lovingly to let them know you aren't going to abandon them. Offer them comfort—if they don't take it, let them complete their tantrum without shaming them or telling them they're wrong.

Friendships & Communication

Without SSPA: Feeling unworthy leads to either isolation and withdrawal or love-bombing and people-pleasing.

With SSPA: You affirm your value and show up fully in friendships.

Benefit: More fulfilling friendships, connections and belonging. More energy for yourself and more time filling your own cup first.

Overcoming Fear of Judgment

Thought: *Everyone here is judging me.*

Stop: Catch the social anxiety before it affects your energy.

Swap: Imagine a cat wearing roller skates.

Get Present: Ground yourself by noticing three things around you with your senses.

Action: Initiate a simple conversation by asking someone about their interests or recent experiences. Remind yourself you're safe.

Handling Conflict Calmly

Thought: *I need to defend myself.*

Stop: Notice the tension rising before reacting.

Swap: Imagine a sloth smiling and slowly waving.

Get Present: Take a slow breath before responding. Follow the breath; feel its temperature as it enters and leaves your body.

Action: Respond with curiosity rather than defensiveness. Ask, 'Can you help me understand your perspective?'

Healing & Growth

Without SSPA: Believing you're 'stuck' keeps you from healing.

With SSPA: You reframe struggles as stepping stones to growth.

Benefit: Emotional freedom, resilience and deep healing.

Letting Go of Past Hurt

Thought: *I'll never move on from this pain.*

Stop: As soon as you have the thought, cancel it out with a swap.

Swap: Imagine a duck in a tiny raincoat.

Get Present: Focus on one thing in the moment that makes you feel safe or happy. If you're thinking about the past, you aren't in the now.

Action: Write down one lesson you learned from the past experience. How can it serve your future growth? When we find the lesson in the pain, we can ease it away.

Health

Without SSPA: Negative self-talk causes unhealthy habits, stress and long-term trauma responses. It can affect physical well-being.

With SSPA: You focus on progress and make better health choices.

Benefit: Better physical health, motivation and self-care.

Breaking the Cycle of Emotional Eating

Thought: *I need junk food to feel better.*

Stop: Notice the craving and the emotion behind it.

Swap: Imagine a koala hugging you.

Get Present: Drink a glass of water and stretch your body.

Action: Choose a nourishing snack and acknowledge that you deserve to treat your body with care.

Managing Chronic Pain

Thought: *This will never get better.*

Stop: Notice the frustration before it takes over.

Swap: Picture a dolphin leaping through a doughnut.

Get Present: Focus on the sensation of wiggling your fingers and toes.

Action: Practise gentle body movement, relaxing each muscle group from head to toe. Focus on the parts of you that are particularly vibrant and healthy.

Skipping the Gym

Thought: *I don't feel like working out.*

Stop: Catch the excuse immediately.

Swap: Picture a pink kangaroo with boxing gloves.

Get Present: Get into the moment. (Remember, if you don't want to do something in the present, it means your mind is in the past or future.)

Action: Commit to five minutes of physical activity and let the momentum carry you forward. If you need to start smaller, move your body for just one minute. Then see how you feel.

Legacy & Purpose

Without SSPA: Feeling lost leads to aimlessness.

With SSPA: You affirm your path and take aligned steps.

Benefit: Clarity, motivation and a meaningful life journey. Health, wealth, prosperity and love.

Overcoming Guilt

Thought: *I should have done better.*

Stop: Notice the guilt before it becomes self-criticism and weighs you down.

Swap: Imagine a sleepy kitten in a basket.

Get Present: Breathe deeply and say, 'I did my best with what I knew.'

Action: Do something small that represents your willingness to forgive yourself. In more serious situations, seek out a trauma-informed therapist.

Mental Health

Without SSPA: Anxious or depressive thoughts spiral into emotional overwhelm.

With SSPA: You intercept negative patterns before they affect your mood.

Benefit: Emotional regulation, mental clarity and inner stability.

Managing Anxiety

Thought: *Something bad is going to happen.*

Stop: Catch the worry before it spirals.

Swap: Picture a hamster stuffing its cheeks.

Get Present: Feel your feet on the ground. Name three things you can see. (Anxiety is all about what *could* happen. This means that your thoughts are in the future and formed around current make-believe.)

Action: Tell yourself, 'I'm here in the now and everything is peaceful.' Shine a light into your heart and ask for ease out loud.

Personal Development

Without SSPA: Self-doubt slows growth and keeps you stuck.

With SSPA: You shift into a growth mindset and take action.

Benefit: Faster progress, confidence and a fulfilling journey.

Beating Imposter Syndrome

Thought: *I don't belong here.*

Stop: Catch the self-doubt before it takes root.

Swap: Picture a penguin in a superhero cape.

Get Present: Stand tall, take a deep breath and smile. Name five to ten things around you.

Action: Tell yourself, 'I'm purpose-built, deserve to be here and proudly claim my space.'

Recreation & Fun

Without SSPA: Feeling guilty about fun leads to burnout.

With SSPA: You embrace joy as a necessary part of life.

Benefit: More balance, fulfilment and vitality. The happier and more in love you are, the more open you are to receiving abundance.

Releasing Resentment

Thought: *They always treat me unfairly during activities.*

Stop: Catch the frustration before it builds.

Swap: Imagine a raccoon bouncing around in moon boots.

Get Present: Exhale deeply and let the tension seep out of you.

Action: Write down a single sentence about the resentment you're feeling. Rip it up and throw it away.

Relationships

Without SSPA: Assumptions and negative thoughts cause unnecessary conflict.

With SSPA: You choose understanding and compassion.

Benefit: Stronger connections, better communication and emotional harmony.

Avoiding an Argument with a Partner

Thought: *They never listen to me.*

Stop: Catch the assumption before reacting emotionally.

Swap: Picture a sea lion sliding on ice.

Get Present: Focus on your breath, listening actively.

Action: Take a pause before responding. Ask, 'What are they really trying to express?' Respond with curiosity instead of frustration.

Handling Criticism

Thought: *They think I'm a failure.*

Stop: Pause before letting the assumption take over.

Swap: Picture a room full of brightly coloured balloons.

Get Present: Take a long, slow breath to get back to the 'here and now'.

Action: Reflect on the feedback objectively. What can you learn from it? What can you let go of?

Self-Confidence & Self-Love

Without SSPA: Negative self-talk damages self-esteem.

With SSPA: You shift to self-empowerment and worthiness.

Benefit: Greater confidence, self-acceptance and inner peace.

Halting Negative Self-Talk in the Mirror

Thought: *I look awful today.*

Stop: Catch the self-criticism before it affects your mood.

Swap: Picture a frilly daffodil with a tall party hat.

Get Present: Smile at yourself, touch your heart and say something kind to yourself.

Action: Write down three things you appreciate about yourself.

Stopping Over-Apologizing

Thought: *I'm always in the way.*

Stop: Catch the self-criticism before it affects your mood.

Swap: Picture a blue elephant wearing a tutu.

Get Present: Stand still and own your space.

Action: Practise replacing 'I'm sorry' with 'Thank you for your patience.'

Sexuality & Intimacy

Without SSPA: Insecurity and shame create disconnection.

With SSPA: You embrace self-acceptance and deeper connection.

Benefit: More fulfilling intimacy, confidence and emotional safety.

Bedroom Challenges

Thought: *I'm not attractive enough; my partner must not really want me.*

Stop: Recognize the spiral of insecurity before it builds distance between you and your partner.

Swap: Imagine a warm light surrounding you, reminding you of your worth.

Get Present: Take a deep breath, focus on the moment and allow yourself to feel loved and connected.

Action: Share a vulnerable truth with your partner and invite open communication.

Spirit-Nurturing Practises

Without SSPA: Doubt disrupts consistency and depth of practise.

With SSPA: You trust the process and stay present.

Benefit: Deeper spiritual growth, connection and inner stillness.

Doubting Effectiveness

Thought: *I'm not doing this right; maybe it's not working.*

Stop: Notice the doubt before it pulls you away.

Swap: Picture a glittery, delectable cupcake.

Get Present: Take a deep breath and focus on the moment, allowing yourself to simply be.

Action: Commit to five minutes of your practise, trusting that consistency brings results.

Spirituality

Without SSPA: Doubt and comparison disconnect you from your path.

With SSPA: You reaffirm your connection and trust in the process.

Benefit: A deeper sense of purpose, faith and inner peace.

Releasing the Fear of the Future

Thought: *What if everything goes wrong?*

Stop: Catch the worry before it spirals out of control.

Swap: Imagine a giraffe with a long beard.

Get Present: Bring awareness to what's happening right now.

Action: List five things you're grateful for in the present moment.

Time Management

Without SSPA: Stress over time leads to procrastination and inefficiency.

With SSPA: You reframe time as abundant and prioritise effectively.

Benefit: Increased productivity, clarity and ease.

Reducing Overwhelm with a Busy Schedule

Thought: *There's too much to do, I can't handle this.*

Stop: Notice the stress before it turns into inaction.

Swap: Picture a few sloths dancing in a circle.

Get Present: Take a deep breath and follow it. Note how it feels and where it goes. Do this six times, breathing deeper each time.

Action: Break your tasks into small steps and celebrate each completed step, because no task is too minuscule to count as an achievement.

Wealth & Finances

Without SSPA: Scarcity mindset leads to fear-based decisions and financial stress.

With SSPA: You shift into an abundance mindset, improving financial choices.

Benefit: Financial confidence, better decision-making and wealth attraction.

Releasing Money Anxiety

Thought: *I'll never have enough money.*

Stop: Recognise the scarcity mindset.

Swap: Imagine a billy goat smoking a pipe.

Get Present: Express gratitude for what you have, even if it's small.

Action: Take one practical financial action today, no matter how small. Even putting one dollar into a savings account works!

Anxiety Over Bills

Thought: *I can't afford this.*

Stop: Recognise the scarcity mindset.

Swap: Imagine a penguin holding a miniature snowman.

Get Present: Focus on what is around you in the present moment. State the names of five things out loud.

Action: Create a simple budget or payment plan to ease uncertainty.

Thank You: The Journey Onward

Shitting Myself & Doing This Anyway...

That was my thought as I began to type.

I've been procrastinating writing this book for years due to fear, agreements, shame and all the other limiting beliefs we've just covered. The smartest and most liberating thing I did was ask a friend for help: fellow author and incredible writing mentor, Bradley, who held my hand through this whole process (and thank fuck, because otherwise, this would've been just another idea shut down by my communicator body). Through all the excitement and frustration, he was there, guiding me, holding space and letting me vent when I needed it.

Writing this has been both a joy and a relentless taskmaster, kicking my arse and forcing me to apply every modality I know, a love-hate relationship through and through. As you now know, when we have a vision, goal or deep desire, our communicator body comes up to point out where we're out of alignment with what we want.

Well, *all* my shit surfaced while putting this book together.

I faced the memory of failing year eight not once, but twice. The sting of that humiliation still lingered. Then came the fear of judgment: What would people think? Who was *I* to write a book like this? Could I even do it? So much freaking self-doubt and self-loathing I didn't know was there came up, washing over me in waves when I least expected it.

I'm dumb.

Too stupid for this.

Someone will try to call bullshit on what I have to say.

These thoughts hit me hard, but I had a tool that saved me: SSPA.

Every time those 'I can't' feelings arose, I applied my process. I stopped the spiralling thought, swapped it with a ridiculous image, and got present with the 'bird' technique. Then, I took action by continuing to write (even when I knew I'd wind up discarding half of it).

Despite SSPA, this wasn't a graceful project. I complained. I threw tantrums. There were moments when I just wanted to give up. But I kept going, and Bradley was there through it all, reminding me that the only way out is *through*; that I could do this; that my voice mattered.

If you're holding a dream or desire that feels impossible, remember that the resistance you feel is just a signal, not a stop sign. Use it as a compass to show where you're out of sync with the version of yourself that *already* has what you want. And most importantly, *keep going,* even if you have to drag yourself through to the end.

If I can do it, I know you can too.

To every single mentor who taught me, inspired me, loved me, encouraged me—even those who challenged or betrayed me—thank you. Every lesson has been a gift. I'm so grateful for the invaluable opportunities you brought into my life. It's all so perfect.

To my brave, beautiful and ever-yummy mummy, mother, woman, friend, goddess. My unwavering guide and my greatest supporter. You have always believed in me, never allowing me to doubt myself for a second. Your love is a fortress, and your faith in me has been my anchor. Thank you for being my best friend and my light.

To the sexiest man in the universe: my husband, Anthony. My king. My hero. My lover. My bestie. You stepped into my life and healed the wounds other men left behind. With you, I've never felt so safe to love this deeply. Thank you for sweeping in and carrying the boys and me. You're the love story I'd always dreamed of.

To my incredible sons, Jack and Ben: you're my leverage, my why, my what and my how. There are no words to describe the gratitude I feel for being your mother. To be your landing pad, your safe place, and the arms that always get to hold you is the greatest honour of my life. I see your genius! I always have, and I always will.

Thank you to my right-hand man, Bradley. You are more man than most, my friend. It takes big energy to hold all of my energy, and you do it so gracefully. Thank you for holding me, pushing me, kicking my arse and being the best friend, tea maker, writing mentor and co-writer. Thank you for trusting me.

To my circle of friends, my sisters, I never want to do this without you. Suzanne, Shayla, Shani, Laura, Jillian—oh my god, I need a thousand pages to name you all. To the practitioners who have trained in my modalities and to all my clients: I love you!

A big shout-out to my Uncle Peter, who took over the role of Dad when I was ten months old because my real dad left. You taught me that I can be anything I want to be, whenever I want to be. And I am. Thank you.

Thank you to the Romano family. I love you all so much, and I love our capacity to laugh and love so deeply. To my Mornement family: I am me because of you. You are my blood and my heart.

Thank you.

All of you.

For everything.

~ Emma

Footnote of Gratitude

But Even Bigger!

If you'd asked me a year ago about collaborating on a self-help book instead of finishing my sci-fi and horror novels, I would have laughed and suggested some stellar fiction to read instead.

Yet here we are.

I'm astonished by the amazing things that can happen when inspiration guides the *what,* and higher powers handle the *how.* Surrender is the gift we don't know we need. It was through surrender that I found the peace and self-belief to tackle this book while also coaching my bold and beautiful co-author, Emma. It's been one hell of a mutual effort, complete with laughs, breakthroughs, tears (usually in that order) and even a 3 am haunting in an old barn. No, I'm not a ghost now... but I appreciate your concern.

Creation has a way of leading us down profound and unexpected paths. For me, this book was a deep dive into reflection, resilience and discovery. It took on a life of its own, shaping me as much as I shaped it. It demanded I embrace the unknown. *Insisted* I explore lessons that would extend far beyond its pages. Begged me to have patience and remember this wasn't about me.

I'm thrilled by what we've accomplished, and my greatest hope is that we've helped you chase the change you seek because it's you, dear reader, who makes all of this worthwhile.

Some invaluable souls helped me get to the finish line of this project, and so many others supported me from the sidelines.

To my co-author and longtime friend, Emma, who introduced me to the worlds of spirituality, metaphysics and SSPA: *thank you*. Words cannot express my sheer gratitude for how much you've impacted my life and taught me about myself. This has been a blazing journey of self-discovery, where I've become really good at introspection in a remarkably short time. I'm here for it, and I'm here for you always. I can't wait for what we take on next.

To our original publisher, Laura, our editor, Jade, and our designer, Jen: you make a great team. Thank you for helping us shape this book into something beyond what we could have anticipated and for every moment of time you invested in doing so. I'm honoured to have worked alongside you.

To my handsome husband, Simon, my Billy Zane lookalike and favourite Spice Girls addict: you tolerate my introversion and relentless desire for isolated weekends with manuscripts, and I love you *so* much for it. I appreciate your support more than you'll ever know. Living with me hasn't always been easy, and without your willingness to explore better ways, I wouldn't be the person I am today. My life is beautiful because you're in it. Thank you for choosing me.

To my colleague, Mon, who permitted me the space and flexibility to manage multiple projects at the same time: you're one amazing gal. Thank you for seeing the potential in my work, standing by me when things dipped into chaos and for always being the genuine person you are.

To my amazing family, who have cheered me on from across an ocean: I love you and miss you. Thank you for believing in me and reminding me how lucky I am to have such incredible people in my life. Your support means the world.

To the DiNunzio family, who have welcomed me with open arms: thank you for everything you do. From Sunday lunches to dog-sitting to joining us on holidays, you've made Australia an easier place to call home. You're all a blessing.

To every friend I've neglected while working on this book and my business: please forgive me. I miss you and will see you before you know it.

~ Bradley

*'Achieving a goal only changes your life for the moment.
We think we need to change our results, but the results are not
the problem. What we really need to change are the systems
that cause those results.'*
~ James Clear, Atomic Habits

Glossary

Adrenaline

- Also known as epinephrine: a hormone produced by the adrenal glands and released in response to scares, acute stress and triggered trauma responses.

Agreement

- A belief or thought pattern you accept (consciously or unconsciously) that shapes how you see and experience life. These either help you grow or hold you back.

Caudate Nucleus

- A small grey-matter structure in the brain that responds to dopamine and plays a role in brain neuroplasticity, reward, motivation and learning. Especially critical for adaptive behaviours such as suppressing an old habit, changing a plan or adjusting to new rules and procedures.

Cellular Memory

- The integrated unconscious programming recognised and automatically executed on a cellular level, shaped by our habits, emotions and behaviours.

Communicator Body

- A part of you that indicates or reflects what you need to work on, either triggering you or making you want to be very still and inactive.
- The emotional baggage from past hurt.
- It can be triggered by certain situations, leading to reactive and painful patterns.
- *See also: 'Gabriel'.*

Consciousness

- The awareness of your thoughts, feelings and the world around you. It also refers to the greater intelligence that connects all life.

Cortisol

- A steroid hormone produced by the adrenal glands, resulting from stress, trauma responses and negativity.

Dis-Ease

- Any sort of physical, mental or emotional discomfort that manifests as ailments.

Energy

- The invisible force that flows through everything and shapes how you think, feel and experience life.
- Your energy can be calm and focused or scattered and chaotic.

'Gabriel'

- A soft and inviting way to describe your communicator body when it's showing you old, messy habits affecting the elevation of your soul. It works through triggers, patterns, symptoms and the body.
- Pain, shame and other negative emotions rise when its messages are misinterpreted, or until you're ready to reclaim control through resolving pain, trauma and negative belief systems.
- *See also: communicator body.*

God

- The creative intelligence or source of all life.
- This concept transcends religion, embodying infinite creativity, wisdom, universal laws and power.
- *See also: Source.*

Higher Self

- The most loving, wise and *true* version of you.
- It's the part that knows your purpose and guides you toward your best life.
- *See also: spirit.*

Identity

- The story you tell yourself about who you are.
- This includes your beliefs and labels.
- Changing your identity can change your life.

Limiting Belief

- A thought or belief that holds you back.
- These often come from past experiences, trauma or social conditioning, and limit what you think is possible.

Optic Neuritis

- Inflammation of the optic nerve, which connects the eye to the brain, and it can cause sudden vision loss, pain or color changes in one eye. It's often linked to autoimmune conditions like multiple sclerosis, where the immune system mistakenly attacks the nerve's protective coating.

Programming

- The mental habits and emotional reactions you pick up from your environment and experiences.
- You can change these patterns with conscious effort and by working with the unconscious program, such as through hypnosis or any of Emma's work.

Responsibility

External: the state of being accountable for something, whether it's a task, duty or obligation.

Internal: recognising that we have control over how we respond to situations.

While we can't always control what happens to us, we *can* choose our reactions, attitudes and actions.

Shame

- A deep feeling of being flawed or not good enough. If not healed, it can lead to self-sabotage and disconnection.
- The painful feeling arising from the consciousness of something dishonourable, improper, ridiculous, etc., done by oneself or another.

Source

- The origin of all life and consciousness; pure energy, intelligence and creative potential from which everything comes.
- *See also: God.*

Sovereignty

- Being in charge of yourself.
- It means making decisions from your *truth* and not letting others control your thoughts or actions.

SSPA

- The process outlined in this book.
- Emma's simple four-step method to shift your mindset:

  Stop: Catch negative thoughts.

  Swap: Replace them with a neutral or playful image (like a flamingo).

  Presence: Focus on the present moment.

  Action: Take a positive, intentional step forward.

Spirit

- Your eternal, non-physical essence. It's the part of you that connects to the greater universe beyond your body and mind.
- It's the thread of the divine to create you.
- *See also: higher self.*

Trauma

- Emotional or energetic wounds caused by overwhelming experiences, which can affect your thoughts, emotions, behaviours and even body until healed.
- **In psychiatry:** an experience that produces psychological injury or pain.

Unconscious Self

- The hidden part of the mind that runs automatic thoughts and reactions.
- It holds both unprocessed pain and untapped potential.

Vagus Nerve

- The longest and most complex cranial nerve, it contains both sensory and motor fibers that carry signals back and forth between the organs and central nervous system.

Vibration

- Your energetic 'mood' based on what you think and feel.
- Higher vibrations reflect love and joy.
- Lower ones reflect fear and negativity.

Victimhood

- The propensity to remain caged or boxed in by past trauma in order to gain sympathy from others, or to use the continued suffering as an excuse.

References

Abyzov, A., & Vaccarino, F. (2020). Cell lineage tracing and cellular diversity in humans. *Annual Review of Genomics and Human Genetics.* https://doi.org/10.1146/annurev-genom-083118-015241

Ackerman, A., & Puglisi, B. (2017). The emotional wound thesaurus: A writer's guide to psychological trauma. JADD Publishing.

Andrews-Hanna, J. R. (2011). The brain's default network and its adaptive role in internal mentation. *The Neuroscientist, 18*(3), 251–270. https://doi.org/10.1177/1073858411403316

Ardalan, A. (2024). New research sheds light on how the brain learns to control attention and flexibly adapt to new environments. *Princeton Neuroscience Institute.* https://pni.princeton.edu/news/2024/new-re-search-sheds-light-how-brain-learns-control-attention-and-flexibly-adapt-new

Bono, F., Mutti, V., Fiorentini, C., & Missale, C. (2020). Dopamine D3 receptor heteromerization: Implications for neuroplasticity and neuroprotection. *Biomolecules, 10*(7), 1016. https://doi.org/10.3390/biom10071016

Brody, G. H., Yu, T., & Shalev, I. (2017). Risky family processes prospectively forecast shorter telomere length mediated through negative emotions. *Health Psychology, 36*(5), 438–444. https://doi.org/10.1037/hea0000443

Cioffi, W. G. (2015). Responsibility. *Journal of Trauma and Acute Care Surgery, 78*(4), 661–670. https://doi.org/10.1097/TA.0000000000000569

Coyne, L. W. (2024, May 20). 4 ways to stop negative thinking. McLean Hospital. https://www.mcleanhospital.org/essential/negative-thinking

Doi, T., Fan, Y., Gold, J. I., & Ding, L. (2020). The caudate nucleus contributes causally to decisions that balance reward and uncertain visual information. *eLife, 9,* e56694. https://doi.org/10.7554/eLife.56694

Fausto, N., & Mead, J. (1989). Regulation of liver growth: Protooncogenes and transforming growth factors. *Laboratory Investigation, 60*(1), 4–13. https://doi.org/10.1007/978-1-4612-0485-5_1

Fink, G. (Ed.). (2000). *Encyclopedia of stress.* Academic Press, *1,* 389-392.

Gray, J. (1992). *Men are from Mars, women are from Venus: A practical guide for improving communication and getting what you want in your relationships.* HarperCollins.

Grahn, J. A., Parkinson, J. A., & Owen, A. M. (2008). The cognitive functions of the caudate nucleus. *Progress in Neurobiology, 86*(3), 141–155. https://doi.org/10.1016/j.pneurobio.2008.09.004

Hawkins, D. R., & Grace, F. (2020). *The map of consciousness explained: A proven energy scale to actualize your ultimate potential.* Hay House.

Hays, E. (2022). Check your pipes: The sewage system of the brain. *MiNDS.* https://www.mindatsinai.com/blog/check-your-pipes-the-sewage-system-of-the-brain

Heymans, S. (2024). Eckhart Tolle's hall of mirrors: A guide to finding your way out. Wipf & Stock Publishers. https://books.google.com.au/books?id=Sv0uEQAAQBAJ

Iffland, B., & Neuner, F. (2016). Trauma and memory. In G. Fink (Ed.), *Stress: Concepts, cognition, emotion, and behavior.* (pp. 161–167). Academic Press. https://doi.org/10.1016/B978-0-12-800951-2.00019-4

Jones, M. G., Khodaverdian, A., Quinn, J. J., Chan, M. M., Hussmann, J. J., Wang, R., Xu, C. A., Weissman, J., & Yosef, N. (2019). Inference of single-cell phylogenies from lineage tracing data using Cassiopeia. *Genome Biology, 21,* 1–16. https://doi.org/10.1186/s13059-020-02000-8

Kempster, S., & Jackson, B. (2021). Leadership for what, why, for whom and where? A responsibility perspective. *Journal of Change Management, 21*(1), 45–65. https://doi.org/10.1080/14697017.2021.1861721

N.A. (2024). Caudate nucleus. *KENHUB.* https://www.kenhub.com/en/library/anatomy/caudate-nucleus

Kishimi, I., & Koga, F. (2019). *The courage to be disliked.* Allen & Unwin.

Kishida, K., Pearce, S., Yu, S., Gao, N., & Ferraris, R. (2017). The life and death of differentiated and dedifferentiated intestinal absorptive and secretory cells. *The FASEB Journal, 31*(1 Suppl.), 878.6. https://doi.org/10.1096/fasebj.31.1_supplement.878.6

Mamat, Z., & Anderson, M. C. (2023). Improving mental health by training the suppression of unwanted thoughts. *Science Advances.* https://doi.org/10.1126/sciadv.adh5292

Maslow, A. H. (1943). A theory of human motivation. *Psychological Review, 50*(4), 370–396.

Ma, X., Yue, Z.-Q., Gong, Z.-Q., Zhang, H., Duan, N.-Y., Shi, Y.-T., Wei, G.-X., & Li, Y.-F. (2017). The effect of diaphragmatic breathing on attention, negative affect, and stress in healthy adults. *Frontiers in Psychology, 8*, 874. https://doi.org/10.3389/fpsyg.2017.00874

McLean Hospital. (2024). 4 ways to stop negative thinking. *McLean Hospital.* https://www.mcleanhospital.org/essential/negative-thinking

Moreland, A. (2024, April 25). *Relationship sovereignty* [Workshop]. https://www.drashleighmoreland.com

Parks, J. (2024, April 24). *Relationship sovereignty* [Workshop]. https://www.thelifeprinciple.com.au

Parmacek, M., & Epstein, J. (2009). Cardiomyocyte renewal. *The New England Journal of Medicine, 361*(1), 86–88. https://doi.org/10.1056/NEJMcibr0903347

Pearce, S., Kishida, K., Yu, S., Gao, N., & Ferraris, R. (2017). The life and death of differentiated and dedifferentiated intestinal absorptive and secretory cells. *The FASEB Journal, 31*. https://doi.org/10.1096/fasebj.31.1_supplement.878.6

Phua, Z. J., MacInnis, R. J., & Jayasekara, H. (2022). Cigarette smoking and risk of second primary cancer: A systematic review and meta-analysis. *Cancer Epidemiology, 78*, 102160. https://doi.org/10.1016/j.canep.2022.102160

Rose, E. (2013). *Metaphysical anatomy: Your body is talking, are you listening? (Vol. 1).* CreateSpace Independent Publishing Platform. ISBN 9781482315820

Salamon, M. (2022). Break free from 3 self-sabotaging ANTs—automatic negative thoughts. *Harvard Women's Health Watch.* https://www.health.harvard.edu/blog/break-free-from-3-self-sabotaging-ants-automatic-negative-thoughts-202211082847

Shinn, F. S. (2013). *The magic path of intuition.* Hay House Inc.

Van der Kolk, B. A. (2014). *The body keeps the score: Brain, mind, and body in the healing of trauma.* Viking.

Ware, S. (2025). There's a speed limit to human thought—and it's ridiculously low. *Live Science.* https://www.livescience.com/health/neuroscience/theres-a-speed-limit-to-human-thought-and-its-ridiculously-low

Wharton, D., Morey, K. C., & Hanner, R. (2021). Maternal inheritance of mitochondrial DNA in mice after inter-species hybridization and 138 generations of backcrossing. *Mitochondrial DNA Part A, 32,* 73–75. https://doi.org/10.1080/24701394.2020.1865940

Zhi Jing Phua, R. J., & Jayasekara, H. (2022). Cigarette smoking and risk of second primary cancer: A systematic review and meta-analysis. *Cancer Epidemiology, 78,* 102160. https://doi.org/10.1016/j.canep.2022.102160 https://www.sciencedirect.com/science/article/pii/S1877782122000650

Author Credentials

Emma Romano

Emma is an internationally recognised self-healing coach, master hypnotherapist, trauma resolve expert and three-time Amazon bestselling author.

Her diverse qualifications span multiple disciplines, including a Diploma of Counselling, Reiki I and II, Master Hypnotherapy and Master NLP Practitioner certifications. As a master timeline therapist, she is the creator and trainer of the Timeline Reset, a groundbreaking approach to healing that has transformed the lives of countless individuals, and Delete Reset, a method designed to shift habits and addictions.

Through the signature coaching program she created and trains others in, the Freedom Protocol, she helps families reconnect and thrive through healing practices that nurture the mind, body and soul. As an International Federation of Hypnosis Certified Trainer, she co-facilitates transformative techniques like Dragon Breathwork (with her son, Jack Romano) and the Relationship Sovereignty program.

She is also the co-creator of Release, Rewire, Inspire, a self-empowerment coaching program, and Soul Business Alignment, which helps individuals align their personal and professional lives with their true purpose.

Additionally, she co-created the Soul Aligned Results program, which offered profound, deep personal transformation.

She is the Founder of Thrive In Life Foundation.

If you'd like to reach out to Emma:

    Website: www.emmaromano.com.au

    TikTok: @emmaromano333

    Instagram: healwithemmaromano

    Linktree: https://linktr.ee/emmaromano1111

    Linkedin: www.linkedin.com/in/emmaromanohypnosuccess

    Facebook: https://www.facebook.com/emma.romano1

Emma has helped thousands of clients overcome emotional and energetic blockages through her unique integrative methods. After being diagnosed with multiple sclerosis in 2014 and facing a future of disability and deterioration, Emma turned inward, leading to the creation of her powerful modalities. Her lived experience fuels her mission to raise the collective frequency by training coaches and practitioners in unconscious reprogramming, spiritual recalibration and energy-based healing.

In *Stop It Swap It*, she brings her signature tools to help readers interrupt emotional spirals, reclaim control and build lasting internal shifts buoyed by soul and spirit.

Bradley Ramacher

Bradley's creativity bridges multiple disciplines, with a foundation in commercial photography and graphic design (Art Institute of Seattle) and creative writing (RMIT).

As the founder of Narrative North, he serves as a creativity relationship expert, writing coach, book coach and certified life coach, guiding clients in overcoming inner blocks, reconnecting with themselves, embracing their creative instincts and aligning their purpose with their soul.

His signature coaching programs, enhanced by Emma Romano's modalities, empower writers, creatives and visionaries to break through mental blocks and refine their craft. His work is backed by practitioner certifications in the Timeline Reset, Relationship Sovereignty and the Freedom Protocol programs.

Bradley is a passionate photographer, and has published *Sand, Surf, and Sea*, a collection of beach photography that captures the beauty of coastal landscapes.

Stop It Swap It precedes several upcoming nonfiction and fiction works by Bradley.

If you'd like to work with Bradley:

    Website: www.narrativenorth.org

    TikTok: bradleyramacher

    Instagram: bradleyramacher

    Linktree: https://linktr.ee/bradleyramacher

Linkedin: www.linkedin.com/in/bradleyramacher
Bluesky: bradleyramacher.bsky.social
Facebook: https://www.facebook.com/bramacher

~

Bradley helps individuals dismantle limiting beliefs and reconnect with their power to create.

He discovered the power of mental and spiritual transformation through his former work in mental health advocacy and after his own battles with anxiety, depression, homosexuality, ADHD and alcoholism.

His reinvention from self-doubt to soul-centred creation became the foundation of his coaching practice and part of the inspiration behind *Stop It Swap It*.

He specialises in bringing order to chaos and blending storytelling with intuition to support profound, lasting change.